EASY VEGAN COMFORT FOOD

Easy VEGAN COMFORT FOOD

80 FAVORITES MADE VEGAN IN 5 STEPS OR LESS

BARB MUSICK

PHOTOGRAPHY BY KATE SEARS

ROCKRIDGE
PRESS

For general information on our other products and services or to obtain technical support, please contact our Customer Care Department within the United States at (866) 744-2665, or outside the United States at (510) 253-0500.

Rockridge Press publishes its books in a variety of electronic and print formats. Some content that appears in print may not be available in electronic books, and vice versa.

Interior and Cover Designer: Eric Pratt
Art Producer: Sara Feinstein
Editor: Van Van Cleave
Production Manager: Riley Hoffman
Production Editor: Melissa Edeburn

Photography © 2020 Kate Sears
Food styling by Lori Powell
Author photo courtesy of Angela Prodanova

ISBN: Print 978-1-64876-006-8 | eBook 978-1-64876-007-5
R0

FOR THE VEGANS, VEGETARIANS, AND EVERYONE
EATING MORE PLANT-BASED MEALS—THE ANIMALS
AND THE PLANET THANK YOU!

CONTENTS

INTRODUCTION

I celebrated my 10-year "veganniversary" while writing this book, which was a very exciting milestone for me. I've been an animal lover my entire life. As a child, I was always bringing home wounded chipmunks and birds and asking my mom to let us adopt (another) dog or cat. When I was five or six years old, we lived near a small family-owned dairy farm, and I considered every single one of the cows my friends. I spent many afternoons lounging and playing in the pasture with them.

It wasn't until I was in high school that I began to view my love of some animals and my willingness to eat others as problematic. At that time, there were no vegetarian adults in my life I could turn to for guidance. In my late teens and early twenties, I had a few failed attempts at going vegetarian, but I always felt stymied by a lack of information and vegetarian alternative products in the stores. I made a successful transition to a vegetarian diet when I was 30, and two years later I made the jump to veganism. I've never looked back. It's the best thing I've done for the animals, for the planet, and for myself.

Because I'm vegan for the animals, I decided it would be okay if I had to go without some of my favorite comfort foods. And 10 years ago, there were foods that I just couldn't have: mac 'n' cheese, ranch dressing, creamy soups . . . delicious plant-based versions of these foods just didn't seem to exist. Since then, the world has become much more vegan-friendly. From local vendors to tech start-ups to national brand names, everyone seems to be jumping into the plant-based marketplace. Tasty, compassionate versions of the foods I thought I could no longer eat are popping up everywhere, and I love it. I'm especially excited about what this development means for people who, like me, crave their old comfort foods. Plant-based versions of most animal products are now widely available and easy to find—or to make yourself!—which opens a world of possibilities.

Vegan food isn't typically associated with comfort food. In fact most people see it as the exact opposite: just steamed kale and raw carrots.

Unfortunately, many vegan versions of classic comfort food go too far in the other direction, adding tons of steps and extra ingredients to compensate for the lack of meat. But not the recipes in this book! These comfort food dishes rely on the inherently delicious taste of vegetables, fruits, and grains. Many of the recipes, like Spicy Guacamole (page 36) and Baked Buffalo Cauliflower (page 28), require hardly any work to yield rich and satisfying flavors.

Vegans deserve comforting foods that aren't overly difficult to make and don't require unfamiliar ingredients. That desire led me to start my blog *That Was Vegan?* in 2011. The vision for my blog was always "easy, vegan versions of the comfort foods you miss," a vision that's echoed in this book.

Of course, the foods we find comforting can depend on where we are from. I grew up in New England and so many of my favorite, most craveable dishes include (or are smothered in) maple syrup. I'm also a sucker for a thick, hearty chowder (like Bacon-Potato Chowder, page 64). That said, I've tried to include traditional comfort food from a variety of regions that I think will appeal to everyone. Every recipe in this book has made me happy, and I hope every one of them will make you happy, too!

CHAPTER ONE

VEGANIZED COMFORTS

• • • • • • • • • •

Our memories are often intertwined with food. The aroma of a favorite dish can pull us back in time and comfort us like a hug. Most of us have memories of the comfort food we enjoyed throughout our lives, and it's only normal that we still crave those dishes, even if they are made with ingredients we no longer eat. The good news is that nearly every recipe can easily be veganized!

FOR THE LOVE OF PLANTS

When I first decided to go vegan, I thought my love of food and cooking would have to take a backseat to my newfound lifestyle. I thought it would be too hard or that the food would be bland. But, wow, was I wrong! Fresh fruits and vegetables are incredibly tasty in their own right. Close your eyes and imagine the first bite of a perfectly ripe apple on a crisp autumn day or the way your kitchen smells when you have veggies roasting in the oven. Amazing, right? But eating vegan isn't just about the sublime foods we get to enjoy; it's also about our health and the health of the planet. Plant-based ingredients, with their fresh flavors and tantalizing textures, are also full of vitamins, minerals, protein, and fiber. A balanced diet of whole grains, legumes, fruits, and veggies has everything your body needs to stay healthy and strong. Eating vegan is also one of the biggest contributions you as an individual can make to help fight climate change. I call that a win-win-win!

FEEL-GOOD FOODS

Food has always been a source of comfort to me, and I know I'm not alone. Most of us, no matter what part of the world we are from, have our own versions of comfort food—a dish or meal that is important to us, that calms us, that lifts our spirits. I also think "comfort food" goes beyond just re-creating those memories. There are certain tastes and textures that we find intensely satisfying, even while the exact flavor profiles vary. A warm, hearty stew is an uplifting dish no matter how you make it. Whether it's full of savory root vegetables or spicy green chiles, a stew is served in a bowl you can wrap your hands around, breathe in the scent, and instantly feel better. Comfort foods can be sweet, too! The flavor combination of peanut butter and chocolate is something that speaks to me. I'll let them melt together in my mouth, and suddenly I feel more centered.

If you're like me and weren't raised vegan, then it's likely that your comfort foods aren't plant-based. But that doesn't mean you've said goodbye to them forever! Vegans today have plentiful, plant-based cheese and meat options to choose from; and with specialty and international shops as well as online resources, we can source even the most hard-to-find ingredients. So, while French fries are thankfully vegan, rest assured that whether you're hankering for Fettuccine Alfredo (page 84) or French Bread Pizza (page 75), they can be made the vegan way!

Times of Comfort

Whether comfort foods are hot or cold, smothered in gooey cheese or rich tomato sauce, they all have one thing in common: They make us feel better. If you're looking for that one, perfect comfort food to fit your mood, here are some suggestions:

Winter Day: It's cold out, and maybe the wind is howling. If warm and soothing is what you're looking for, try the rich and creamy Broccoli-Cheddar Soup (page 58).

Thanksgiving: Forget the "vegan roasts"; my favorite Thanksgiving dish is always Baked Mac 'n' Cheese (page 105)! It's the ultimate cheesy indulgence, and everyone loves it.

Sickness: Chick'n Noodle Soup (page 59) is the plant-based "cure" for whatever ails you. Veggies and noodles and so much flavor will help clear away any cold.

Love: Want to show a loved one how special they are? Start their day off right with an amazing breakfast like Blueberry-Cinnamon Monkey Bread (page 18) or a hearty Veggieful Tofu Scramble (page 23) with a side of toast and fresh fruit!

Feeling Down: We tend to associate certain foods with social gatherings and people taking care of us. When we need a pick-me-up, we look to foods like Deconstructed Lasagna (page 89) to call to mind memories of times we felt secure and loved.

EASY AS 1-2-3

I find solace in my kitchen. The small, simple acts of chopping vegetables or stirring a simmering sauce slow me down and make me feel present. So, while I *can* go to the store and buy frozen vegan lasagna, I find it more emotionally fulfilling and healthier to make my own. I promise it doesn't have to be difficult! I've designed the recipes in this book to be five steps or fewer and made with easy-to-find ingredients. That way preparing your food is as easy as it is gratifying to eat.

IN THE VEGAN KITCHEN

With the right tools and simple ingredients, comfort foods are back on the menu! I prefer to focus on recipes that aren't too complicated, with easily accessible ingredients. Whether you've been vegan for years or are just starting to experiment with plant-based cooking, it's likely you already have most, if not all, of these things in your kitchen already.

Equipment Must-Haves

I'm usually slow to adopt the "latest and greatest" food gadgets, preferring instead to stick with straightforward, quality tools that serve more than one purpose. You'll notice throughout this book that there are no special or unusual tools called for in the recipes. Here are five trusty kitchen items I own and use almost daily.

BLENDER: This is an essential tool for blending sauces, pureeing soups, and making most oat and nut milks. There are a range of different blenders for every budget, and a standard upright or immersion blender will work for the recipes in this book.

FOOD PROCESSOR: A processor is great tool for quickly and easily chopping vegetables, crumbling seitan, and turning cashews into ricotta cheese. But if you have a powerful blender, you can use that instead.

FINE-MESH SIEVES: These come in handy for basic tasks like draining and rinsing a can of beans, but also for more advanced recipes like making Simple Oat Milk (page 140).

BAKING DISHES: These are a must-have for creating comfort foods like Crispy Potato Hotdish (page 118) and Loaded Baked Potato Casserole (page 50). You don't need one in every size, but having at least one small, medium, and large baking dish will be most convenient.

QUALITY KNIVES: A dull knife is more likely to injure you than a sharp one, and quality knives will hold their edges longer. I recommend stainless steel or ceramic-coated blades, as they can go a while without needing sharpening (but still remember to sharpen them regularly!).

Pantry Essentials

I love being able to make my own vegan substitutions such as Cool 'n' Creamy Vegan Sour Cream (page 136) and Zesty Vegan Ranch Dressing (page 145), and I encourage you to try your hand at those as well. But I also know that sometimes, buying these products is the more realistic option. Either way you go, here are a few of the reliable products I keep on hand and I recommend you do, too.

CASHEWS: Raw cashews can be used to make everything from Craveable Cashew Ricotta (page 141) to Zesty Vegan Ranch Dressing (page 145). They also make a delicious, healthy snack.

CHIA SEEDS: Use these seeds to substitute for eggs in your baked dishes (instead of store-bought egg substitutes). Using chia is a more natural approach, and the seeds are easy to find.

DAIRY ALTERNATIVES: From cheese to milk to sour cream, there are myriad vegan dairy products out there. Keep the ones you use most often on hand.

EGG SUBSTITUTES: There are a couple of brands out there, both powdered and liquid, that make baking a breeze.

FROZEN VEGETABLES: Frozen veggies can be added to any recipe you're trying to make more nutritious, and they're very affordable.

KALA NAMAK: This pungent salt (kala namak means "black salt" in Hindi) is a secret ingredient that makes your dishes taste just like eggs.

NUTRITIONAL YEAST: More commonly known as "nooch," this can be added to sauces and scrambles for a cheesy flavor or just sprinkled atop your favorite pasta as you would Parmesan.

OILS: Be sure to buy good-quality oils. I like to use olive oil and avocado oil, along with a more neutral vegetable oil for when I don't want a strong flavor. Tasting the oil is the best way to tell if it is of good quality, but good luck doing that in a grocery store! I recommend avoiding the least expensive bottles, and once you find one you love, stick with it.

SMOKED PAPRIKA: This is the most magical of spices! It gives everything a beautiful smoky flavor that I prefer over liquid smoke.

VEGAN ICE CREAM: Whether it's oat-, cashew-, or soy-based, ice cream is one of the best comfort foods around. Experiment to find your favorite flavor! (Mine is oat-based with peanut butter or caramel!)

VITAL WHEAT GLUTEN: If you want to make your own Mouthwatering Seitan "Meat" (page 147) or, better yet, your own Super Smoky Seitan Bacon (page 149), you'll need to keep this gluten stocked in your pantry.

Simple Shortcuts

When you're really hungry for that comfort food, the last thing you want is a big cooking project. After all, the point of comfort food is to make ourselves feel better, not more stressed, right? Therefore, I am officially giving you permission to take shortcuts with these recipes. Here are a few of my favorite shopping and cooking hacks, designed to make life easier.

◆ Always keep a batch of Mouthwatering Seitan "Meat" (page 147) in your freezer. It's so versatile you can throw it into any dish for an added protein boost.

◆ Give yourself permission to buy pre-cut veggies at the grocery store.

◆ Don't be afraid to lean on frozen produce. Whether its chopped butternut squash or a basic stir-fry mix, frozen veggies are healthy and affordable and will save you a lot of time. An important detail to keep in mind is that the veggies are usually blanched before being frozen, which means they need less time to cook than their fresh counterparts. If you use frozen veggies in a recipe, subtract 2 to 4 minutes from the stated cook time and keep an eye on them so they don't get overcooked.

◆ Except for baked desserts, don't wait for the oven to preheat to start cooking. I roast veggies often, and I'll always put them in the oven right away, so I'm combining a few minutes of roasting with the preheat process. I find that, as a rule of thumb, every 5 minutes in a preheating oven equals 2 to 3 in a fully heated one.

◆ Save small containers and repurpose them to hold homemade spice mixes (think Italian or fajita blends). Choose the ones you use most often and prepare them yourself to save time and money.

ABOUT THE RECIPES

The recipes in this book all speak to me, and they all say the same thing: We're indulgent and delicious. Every recipe was written to provide joy and comfort, to ease sadness and stress. Some are more veggie-forward, whereas others are all-out calorie fests—and that's okay! Breakfast Anytime will offer decadent morning meals along with healthy starts, while Snack Attacks gives you fun, yet simple ways to satisfy a craving. Noodles for Days has all our favorite noodle dishes, from Vegetable Lo Mein (page 88) to a Deconstructed Lasagna (page 89) that is easy enough to make on a weeknight, and Deep-Dish Bakes is full of comforting casseroles. I hope you find recipes that call out to you. Recipes you just cannot resist—and why try to?

We all deserve comfort, and I hope the dishes in this book help you find yours. And don't forget about the DIY Staples chapter, full of recipes for some of the most common vegan alternatives. For my avid DIY-ers, all vegan ingredients called for in this book—such as bacon, cream cheese, sour cream, butter, and milk—have homemade alternatives, so that you can make every recipe truly from scratch if you choose. The one exception is cheese: See What's the Deal with Cheese? (page 9).

What's the Deal with Cheese?

You may notice there aren't any recipes for vegan cheese in the DIY chapter, and there is a good reason for that. Homemade vegan cheeses (especially the harder, shreddable cheeses that are called for in the recipes in this book) can be difficult and time-consuming to make. Some require days of fermentation and call for ingredients that can be difficult to find.

There are so many delicious vegan cheeses on the market now, in a wide variety of flavors (mozzarella, Gouda, pepper jack, even good old "American," which takes me back to the cheese sandwiches of my youth!). They come in blocks, slices, and shreds and are both easy to find and easy to use in all your favorite recipes. While I know many readers may prefer to make their own vegan cheese at home (and I tip my cap to you!), in keeping with the "easy" theme of this book, I felt it would be better to focus on the varieties that can be purchased in stores and online.

If store-bought cheeses are new to you, here are a few of my favorite brands to get you started:

Shredded: Violife and Daiya both melt wonderfully. The mozzarella from either brand is perfect on pizza!

Sliced and blocks: Follow Your Heart, Chao, and Violife are my favorites. I especially recommend Violife Smoked Provolone—it's life-changing!

Soft: Miyoko's makes cheese wheels and spreadable cheese dips that are great for entertaining, and WayFare makes queso dips in a couple different flavors that are all delicious.

Miscellaneous: Violife makes feta and Parmesan cheeses. But when it comes to Parmesan, don't forget about nutritional yeast, which is excellent sprinkled over your favorite pasta dish. Also note that Trader Joe's and Whole Foods each has a growing line of vegan cheeses you can check out.

There are many more brands (with new flavors being launched all the time), so have fun taste-testing until you find your favorite!

Lastly, I've also included tips with each recipe. Some tips help you prepare parts of the recipes ahead of time. Some offer ideas for variations, to change up the dish in tasty ways. Others are designed to help you make the recipe a little healthier, whether that means fewer calories or less sodium. And speaking of healthy, I have also included labels on the recipes to help readers decide if a dish will meet special dietary needs. Because there are so many different variations of vegan products available, the labels are often presented as options. I will explain more below about what these specific "options" mean, but it's good practice to always read the labels of your store-bought products, especially if you have any intolerances or allergies.

GLUTEN-FREE/GLUTEN-FREE OPTION: A recipe labeled "gluten-free" does not have any known sources of gluten. (If you or someone you're cooking for needs to avoid gluten, you are probably already familiar with all those sources.) If a recipe is labeled "gluten-free option," it means that although no obvious forms of gluten (such as flour and bread) have been used, you must still check to ensure that any of the other ingredients do not contain any hidden gluten. This also holds true for things like oats, which are often cross-contaminated, so look for those that are certified gluten-free.

NUT-FREE/NUT-FREE OPTION: A recipe will be labeled "nut-free option" when a dairy alternative is called for. Numerous choices are made with coconut, soy, oats, and rice. (Check out my tofu-based Alfredo Sauce on page 142. It is so creamy!)

SOY-FREE/SOY-FREE OPTION: If you're avoiding soy, then tofu and tempeh are off the menu, but you can still enjoy my Mouthwatering Seitan "Meat" (page 147)! As with nuts, many dairy alternatives are made with soy, so a recipe labeled "soy-free option" indicates you should seek out a soy-free version of the "dairy" ingredient listed, such as nut-, oat-, rice-, or coconut-based products.

And now, it's time for the recipes! I've enjoyed making every dish in this book, and I hope they bring you comfort, calm, and happiness.

BLUEBERRY-CINNAMON MONKEY BREAD · 18

CHAPTER TWO

BREAKFAST ANY TIME

. . . .

STRAWBERRY-BANANA PARFAIT BOWLS

SERVES 4 / **PREP TIME:** 10 minutes / **COOK TIME:** 4 minutes
GLUTEN-FREE OPTION / **NUT-FREE OPTION** / **SOY-FREE OPTION**

If you're looking for a fancy breakfast that also happens to be a cinch to make and nutritious, look no further. These bowls are an easy and delicious starter for first-time vegan cooks. For additional decadence, top them with Sweet Tooth Coconut Whipped Cream (page 137).

FOR THE COMPOTE

1½ cups strawberries

1 tablespoon real maple syrup

2 teaspoons chia seeds

1 teaspoon vanilla extract

¼ teaspoon salt

FOR THE PARFAIT BOWLS

2 cups vegan vanilla yogurt

2 cups granola, your favorite

1 large banana, sliced

Sliced strawberries, for topping

Coconut whipped cream, for topping
(optional)

1. Heat a small saucepan over medium heat. Add the strawberries, maple syrup, chia seeds, vanilla, and salt and stir until combined. Cook for 3 to 4 minutes, stirring frequently, until the berries are broken down and the entire mixture is saucy. Remove from the heat and let cool until just barely warm.

2. Spoon the compote into 4 bowls or glasses. Dividing evenly, top each with a layer of yogurt and granola. Top with the banana and strawberry slices and a dollop of coconut whipped cream, if desired.

   VARIATION: Raspberries and blackberries can be substituted for some or all the strawberries.

VANILLA-BERRY BAKED OATMEAL

SERVES 8 / PREP TIME: 10 minutes / **COOK TIME:** 40 minutes
GLUTEN-FREE OPTION / NUT-FREE OPTION / SOY-FREE OPTION

This hearty breakfast can power you through even the longest day. It is a go-to for me before a brisk fall hike and on chilly winter mornings when I feel like I need something extra robust. Use any berries you like or have on hand; they will all pair well with vanilla and oats.

Nonstick cooking spray

4 tablespoons vegan butter

1 large banana

1¾ cups unsweetened nondairy milk

⅓ cup real maple syrup

⅓ cup unsweetened applesauce

3 cups rolled oats

3 tablespoons light brown sugar

2 teaspoons vanilla extract

1 teaspoon baking powder

1 teaspoon ground cinnamon

¼ teaspoon salt

1½ cups berries, your choice

Vegan vanilla yogurt, for topping (optional)

Additional berries, for topping (optional)

1. Preheat the oven to 350°F. Lightly mist a 2-quart baking dish with cooking spray. Melt the butter in a microwave-safe container.

2. In a large bowl, mash the banana with a fork. Mix in the melted butter, milk, maple syrup, applesauce, oats, brown sugar, vanilla, baking powder, cinnamon, salt, and berries.

3. Pour the mixture into the baking dish and bake for 35 to 40 minutes, until the center is just barely soft and almost set. Let cool for a few minutes before serving.

MAKE AHEAD: Refrigerate the leftovers in an airtight container for up to 5 days.

DIY: Make your own butter (page 146) and milk (page 140).

BLUEBERRY 'N' OATS MUFFINS

SERVES 4 / PREP TIME: 15 minutes, plus 20 minutes to soak / **COOK TIME:** 30 minutes
NUT-FREE OPTION / SOY-FREE OPTION

Muffins are the original portable breakfast and make excellent snacks. Blueberries are full of iron and calcium and help keep your bones strong. A match made in heaven! If you want to pump up the fiber, substitute whole-wheat flour for up to ½ cup of the all-purpose flour.

Nonstick cooking spray

1 cup rolled oats

1 cup unsweetened nondairy milk

1¼ cups all-purpose flour

1 teaspoon baking powder

½ teaspoon baking soda

½ teaspoon ground cinnamon

½ teaspoon salt

¼ teaspoon ground nutmeg

1 large banana

8 tablespoons vegan butter, melted

½ cup real maple syrup

1½ teaspoons vanilla extract

1 cup blueberries

1. Preheat the oven to 350°F. Lightly coat a 12-cup muffin tin with cooking spray.

2. In a bowl, stir together the oats and milk and set aside for about 20 minutes. The oats should be slightly puffy from soaking up the milk.

3. In a large bowl, whisk together the flour, baking powder, baking soda, cinnamon, salt, and nutmeg.

4. In another bowl, use the back of a fork to mash the banana, then whisk in the melted butter, maple syrup, and vanilla. Pour the wet mixture into the dry ingredients and stir to combine. Gently fold in the oats (with any remaining milk) and the blueberries.

5. Pour or spoon the batter into the muffin tin, filling each cup to the top. Bake for 25 to 30 minutes, until the tops are firm to the touch and a toothpick inserted into the center comes out clean. Transfer the muffins to a wire rack to cool before serving.

MAKE AHEAD: Refrigerate the muffins in an airtight container for up to 5 days.

DIY: Make your own milk (page 140) and butter (page 146).

BLUEBERRY-CINNAMON MONKEY BREAD

SERVES 8 / **PREP TIME:** 15 minutes / **COOK TIME:** 45 minutes
NUT-FREE OPTION / **SOY-FREE OPTION**

It may have a silly name, but this decadent dish is perfect for brunch or a holiday breakfast. Kids love it, so get them in the kitchen to help make it.

Nonstick cooking spray

½ cup granulated sugar

1½ teaspoons ground cinnamon

4 (7.5-ounce) cans refrigerated vegan biscuits, each biscuit cut into 4 pieces

1½ cups blueberries

6 tablespoons vegan butter, melted

½ cup packed light brown sugar

1 teaspoon vanilla extract

1. Preheat the oven to 350°F. Lightly mist a full-size Bundt pan with cooking spray.

2. In a bowl, combine the granulated sugar and cinnamon. Working in batches, toss the biscuit pieces in the sugar mixture until coated, transferring them to the Bundt pan as you go. Pour the blueberries into the pan, poking some down in between the pieces of biscuit. Sprinkle the remaining cinnamon-sugar mixture over the top.

3. In a small bowl, whisk together the melted butter, brown sugar, and vanilla. Pour over the top of the biscuits and blueberries.

4. Bake for 40 to 45 minutes, until the top is a light golden brown and feels firm to the touch. Let cool for 10 minutes, then invert onto a serving platter. Cut and serve warm.

VARIATION: Feel like strawberries instead of blueberries? Use the same amount of sliced strawberries, reduce the cinnamon to 1 teaspoon, and increase the vanilla to 2 teaspoons.

DIY: Make your own butter (page 146).

MAPLE-BACON FRENCH TOAST SKEWERS

SERVES 4 / **PREP TIME:** 20 minutes / **COOK TIME:** 15 minutes
NUT-FREE OPTION / **SOY-FREE OPTION**

Whether you're serving these skewers at brunch or enjoying them alone in your pajamas, the salty-sweet combination of maple and bacon cannot be beat.

1 banana

1½ cups unsweetened nondairy milk

1 teaspoon vanilla extract

½ teaspoon ground cinnamon

2 to 3 tablespoons vegan butter, divided

6 slices (½-inch-thick) day-old
   French bread

8 to 12 slices vegan bacon

⅓ cup real maple syrup

1. In a mixing bowl, mash the banana with a fork. Whisk in the milk, vanilla, and cinnamon until smooth.

2. Heat a large skillet over medium heat and melt just enough butter to coat the pan. Dip two slices of bread into the milk mixture until both sides are completely coated and place in the hot pan. Cook each side for 3 to 4 minutes, or until light golden brown. Repeat with the remaining bread.

3. Reheat the bacon according to the package directions and cut it into 1- to 2-inch pieces. Cut the French toast slices into 4 to 6 pieces, roughly the same size as the bacon pieces.

4. Slide the French toast pieces onto wooden skewers, alternating 2 or 3 pieces of bacon for every 1 piece of French toast. Heat the maple syrup and 1 tablespoon butter together in a ramekin and serve alongside the skewers for dipping.

VARIATION: If you don't want the banana flavor, you can substitute 1 vegan egg of your choice and reduce the milk to 1¼ cups.

DIY: Make your own milk (page 140), butter (page 146), and bacon (page 149). If using homemade bacon, reheat it in the microwave for 30 to 45 seconds.

APPLE CRISP FRENCH TOAST CASSEROLE

SERVES 6 / PREP TIME: 15 minutes **/ COOK TIME:** 1 hour
NUT-FREE OPTION / SOY-FREE OPTION

This delectable baked French toast brings a little bit of dessert to breakfast, so I recommend serving it on special occasions like holidays and birthdays. I made this for my mom on Mother's Day and she was over the moon!

FOR THE FRENCH TOAST CASSEROLE

Nonstick cooking spray

1½ cups unsweetened nondairy milk

½ cup unsweetened applesauce

¼ cup real maple syrup, plus more
  for serving

1 teaspoon vanilla extract

1 teaspoon ground cinnamon

¼ teaspoon salt

5 cups cubed day-old French bread

2 medium apples, peeled, cored,
  and chopped

FOR THE TOPPING

⅓ cup rolled oats

⅓ cup all-purpose flour

¼ cup packed light
  brown sugar

4 tablespoons cold vegan butter,
  plus more for serving

¼ teaspoon ground cinnamon

⅛ teaspoon salt

1. Preheat the oven to 350°F. Lightly coat a 1½-quart baking dish with cooking spray.

2. In a large bowl, whisk together the milk, applesauce, maple syrup, vanilla, cinnamon, and salt. Add the bread and apples and toss until completely coated. Pour the entire mixture into the baking dish.

3. In a separate bowl, make the topping by combining the oats, flour, brown sugar, butter, cinnamon, and salt. Use a pastry cutter or your fingers to pinch and mix the dry ingredients with the butter until the butter is broken down into pea-sized pieces. Scatter the crumble mixture on top of the apple mixture in the baking dish.

4. Bake for 50 to 60 minutes, until the top is golden brown and the edges are bubbling. Serve warm with maple syrup and vegan butter.

MAKE AHEAD: This casserole can be assembled the night before for an even faster morning preparation. Assemble everything in the baking dish (except the topping), cover, and refrigerate. Store the topping separately and add it right before baking.

DIY: Make your own milk (page 140) and butter (page 146).

VEGGIEFUL TOFU SCRAMBLE

SERVES 4 / PREP TIME: 20 minutes / **COOK TIME:** 10 minutes

GLUTEN-FREE / NUT-FREE OPTION

Kala namak is a black salt that is widely used in Southeast Asian cooking. It has become popular in the vegan community because you can use it to replicate the sulfurous, umami taste of eggs in your cooking. If you don't enjoy that flavor, simply substitute regular salt.

1 tablespoon olive oil

1 bell pepper, any color, roughly diced

½ sweet onion, thinly sliced

½ teaspoon garlic powder

1 Roma (plum) tomato, roughly diced

1 (14-ounce) package firm tofu,
   well pressed

½ teaspoon kala namak

½ teaspoon ground turmeric

⅛ to ¼ teaspoon black pepper

Pinch red pepper flakes (optional)

2 tablespoons unsweetened
   nondairy milk

½ cup shredded vegan Cheddar cheese

1. In a large skillet, heat the oil over medium heat. Add the bell pepper, onion, and garlic powder and sauté for 4 to 5 minutes, just until the veggies start to soften. Add the tomato and cook for another minute or two.

2. Push the veggies to the outer edges of the pan and crumble the tofu into the center. Stir the kala namak, turmeric, black pepper, red pepper flakes (if using), and milk into the tofu until well combined. Then stir the tofu and veggies together.

3. Reduce the heat to low and stir in the cheese. Cover and let cook, stirring occasionally, for 2 to 3 minutes. Add more milk if you want the scramble to be softer. Taste and add additional salt and pepper as desired.

LIGHTEN UP: Use 2 to 4 tablespoons water instead of oil to sauté the veggies. Keep a close watch and add more water as needed so the veggies don't stick to the pan.

DIY: Make your own milk (page 140).

SWEET CORN PANCAKES

SERVES 4 / PREP TIME: 5 minutes **/ COOK TIME:** 8 minutes

NUT-FREE OPTION / SOY-FREE OPTION

I remember my dad making these for me on special occasions when I was a little girl, and they've been a favorite ever since. My dad grew up in Canada and New Hampshire, where this combination of a pancake and a corn fritter was a common treat... although his were the best! Be sure to serve them with plenty of vegan butter and maple syrup.

1¼ cups all-purpose flour

1 teaspoon baking powder

¼ teaspoon baking soda

⅛ teaspoon salt

1 cup unsweetened nondairy milk

2 tablespoons water

1 cup sweet corn

Vegan butter, for greasing pan
     and serving

Real maple syrup, for serving

1. In a large bowl, stir together the flour, baking powder, baking soda, and salt until completely combined. Slowly pour in the milk and water and mix just until smooth. Some very small lumps are okay (be sure not to overmix the batter). Fold in the corn.

2. Heat a skillet over medium-high heat. Melt enough butter to coat the pan. Use a ladle or large spoon to transfer the batter to the pan, about ¼ cup at a time. When bubbles appear and begin to pop (about 2 minutes), flip and cook the pancakes for another 1 to 2 minutes, or until golden brown.

3. Serve with butter and maple syrup.

VARIATION: For a more traditional take, substitute blueberries for the corn. Sprinkle the blueberries on the batter after you've poured it into the pan instead of mixing them together.

DIY: Make your own milk (page 140) and butter (page 146).

SPINACH DIP · 30

CHAPTER THREE

SNACK ATTACKS

· · · ·

BAKED BUFFALO CAULIFLOWER

SERVES 4 / **PREP TIME:** 10 minutes / **COOK TIME:** 25 minutes
GLUTEN-FREE / **NUT-FREE OPTION** / **SOY-FREE OPTION**

This dish is excellent on its own or as a salad topping. Pro tip: Frank's RedHot Buffalo sauce is vegan and my personal favorite.

4 cups cauliflower florets

½ cup Buffalo sauce, plus more
    for serving

¼ teaspoon salt

⅛ teaspoon black pepper

Vegan ranch dressing or vegan blue
    cheese dressing, for serving (optional)

1. Preheat the oven to 375°F.

2. Spread the florets out on a rimmed baking sheet. Cover the florets with the Buffalo sauce and stir until coated. Sprinkle with the salt and pepper.

3. Bake for 20 to 25 minutes, or until tender, stirring halfway through. Let cool for a few minutes. Serve with additional Buffalo sauce and/or dressing, if desired.

MAKE AHEAD: The baked cauliflower will keep in an airtight container in the refrigerator for up to 3 days. For reheating, pop it under a low broiler for 30 to 60 seconds, or until it's hot and a little crispy.

DIY: Make your own ranch dressing (page 145).

CREAMY ROASTED CORN AND GREEN CHILE DIP

SERVES 8 / PREP TIME: 10 minutes / **COOK TIME:** 35 minutes
GLUTEN-FREE / NUT-FREE OPTION / SOY-FREE OPTION

The natural sweetness of roasted corn pairs well with spicy chiles. Control your level of heat by choosing either mild or hot green chiles. Serve this dip with salty corn chips or fresh carrot and celery sticks.

Nonstick cooking spray
1 (12-ounce) bag frozen corn
2 tablespoons olive oil
½ teaspoon salt
½ teaspoon black pepper
½ teaspoon smoked paprika (optional)
1½ cups vegan ricotta cheese

1 (4-ounce) can fire-roasted diced green chiles, drained
1 cup shredded vegan Cheddar or pepper jack cheese
2 tablespoons sliced scallions (optional)
Corn chips or veggie sticks, for serving

1. Preheat the oven to 400° F. Lightly coat a 1½-quart baking dish with cooking spray and set aside.

2. In a bowl, toss the corn with the olive oil, salt, pepper, and smoked paprika (if using). Spread on a rimmed baking sheet in a single layer and bake for 15 to 20 minutes, stirring once halfway, until most pieces have a golden-brown color.

3. Transfer the corn to the baking dish and combine with the ricotta and green chiles. Cover with the shredded cheese and bake for 10 to 15 minutes, until the dip is heated all the way through and the cheese is melted. If desired, top with the scallions. Serve with your favorite corn chips or veggie sticks.

VARIATION: This dip also makes a killer spread! Schmear some on a pita or wrap and add your favorite crisp, fresh veggies.

DIY: Make your own ricotta (page 141).

SPINACH DIP

SERVES 8 / PREP TIME: 10 minutes, plus 1 hour to chill
GLUTEN-FREE OPTION / NUT-FREE OPTION / SOY-FREE OPTION

Before I learned how to cook, my contribution to potlucks was always spinach dip made with a packet of dried soup mix. It was tasty, but this version is even better. Most Worcestershire sauce is made with anchovies, so be sure to seek out a brand that is vegan.

1½ cups vegan sour cream

¾ cup vegan mayonnaise

1½ teaspoons onion powder

1 teaspoon salt

½ teaspoon sweet paprika

¼ teaspoon garlic powder

¼ teaspoon black pepper

1 (16-ounce) package frozen chopped spinach, thawed

2 teaspoons vegan Worcestershire sauce

½ cup sliced scallions

1 (8-ounce) can water chestnuts, drained and diced

Crackers, bread, or raw veggies, for dipping

1. In a large bowl, stir together the sour cream, mayonnaise, onion powder, salt, paprika, garlic powder, and pepper.

2. Squeeze as much liquid as you can from the spinach, then add it to the bowl along with the Worcestershire sauce, scallions, and water chestnuts. Cover and refrigerate for at least 1 hour before serving with crackers, bread, or raw veggies for dipping.

VARIATION: Hollow out a round sourdough loaf to use as a serving bowl and use the chunks of bread to dip with.

DIY: Make your own sour cream (page 136) and mayo (page 139).

MINI FRIED TACOS

SERVES 6 / **PREP TIME:** 15 minutes / **COOK TIME:** 20 minutes
NUT-FREE OPTION / **SOY-FREE OPTION**

This recipe was inspired by a dish known as Navajo Tacos, in which fry bread is used in place of a tortilla. The Arizona Navajo people first made fry bread in 1864, when the U.S. government forced them on the 300-mile "Long Walk" relocation to New Mexico. I encourage you to learn more about this complex history and try making your own fry bread. Here, dinner rolls are substituted as a shortcut.

Nonstick cooking spray

12 frozen yeast dinner rolls, thawed

1 to 2 cups vegetable or canola oil

1 (15.5-ounce) can medium or hot chili beans

1 tomato, diced

½ onion, diced

1 cup chopped iceberg lettuce

Vegan sour cream, for topping

1. Grease your hands with cooking spray and stretch each roll out to about 3 inches wide. Pour 1 inch of vegetable oil into a skillet and heat the oil to 350°F. Use tongs to carefully add the dough. Cook in batches for 2 to 3 minutes on each side, or until they are a golden brown. Let the fried rolls drain on paper towels.

2. Meanwhile, heat the beans in a microwave-safe container.

3. Top each piece of dough with 1 to 2 tablespoons of beans, then sprinkle them with tomato, onion, lettuce, and sour cream. Serve while warm.

VARIATION: Once you have the fried rolls, your topping options are unlimited! If you want to go sweet instead of savory, drizzle them with agave and serve for dessert.

DIY: Make your own sour cream (page 136).

CHILI CHEESE FRIES

SERVES 4 / PREP TIME: 15 minutes / **COOK TIME:** 15 minutes
GLUTEN-FREE OPTION / NUT-FREE OPTION / SOY-FREE OPTION

Chili cheese equals comfort food. These fries are the perfect indulgence for a night spent binge-watching your favorite TV series.

4 cups frozen French fries

2 teaspoons vegetable oil

1 cup vegan crumbles, or
   1 loaf Mouthwatering Seitan "Meat"
   (page 147), crumbled in a food
   processor

1 (15.5-ounce) can mild or hot chili beans

⅓ cup canned tomato puree

2 teaspoons ground cumin

1 teaspoon onion powder

1 teaspoon chili powder

1 teaspoon garlic powder

½ teaspoon salt

¼ teaspoon red pepper flakes

1 cup shredded vegan Cheddar or
   pepper jack cheese

OPTIONAL TOPPINGS

Diced red onions

Sliced scallions

Sliced jalapeños

Vegan sour cream

1. Cook the French fries according to the package directions.

2. In a saucepan, heat the vegetable oil over medium-high heat. Add the vegan crumbles and sauté for 4 to 5 minutes, until lightly browned. Stir in the beans, tomato puree, cumin, onion powder, chili powder, garlic powder, salt, and pepper flakes. Reduce the heat to low and simmer for 5 minutes to warm through.

3. Set the broiler to low. Spread the fries on a broilerproof platter and cover with half the cheese. Broil for 1 to 2 minutes to melt the cheese. Top with the chili and then the remaining cheese, and broil for another 1 to 2 minutes. Serve with your desired toppings.

LIGHTEN UP: Skip the vegan crumbles or seitan and double the amount of chili beans. It's still hearty and filling!

DIY: Make your own sour cream (page 136).

SMOKY CHIPOTLE HUMMUS

SERVES 4 / PREP TIME: 15 minutes
GLUTEN-FREE OPTION / NUT-FREE OPTION / SOY-FREE OPTION

If hummus doesn't strike you as comfort food, you've never had spicy, smoky hummus topped with bacon. Serve this hummus with raw veggies or pretzels.

1 (15-ounce) can chickpeas, drained and liquid reserved
2 chipotle peppers in adobo sauce, plus 1 teaspoon adobo sauce
1 tablespoon tahini

1 teaspoon garlic powder
½ teaspoon salt
¼ teaspoon smoked paprika
6 slices vegan bacon

1. In a food processor or blender, combine the chickpeas, 1 tablespoon of the reserved chickpea liquid, the chipotles, adobo sauce, tahini, garlic powder, salt, and smoked paprika. Blend for about 1 minute or until smooth, periodically pausing to scrape the sides and add more of the chickpea liquid as needed.

2. Spoon the hummus into a serving dish. Dice the bacon and sprinkle on top, then serve chilled or at room temperature.

LIGHTEN UP: To make this healthier, skip the bacon and increase the smoked paprika to 1 teaspoon so you still have that wonderful bacon-y taste.

DIY: Make your own bacon (page 149).

SPICY CAULIFLOWER FRITTERS WITH RANCH DRESSING

SERVES 4 / PREP TIME: 15 minutes / **COOK TIME:** 25 minutes
GLUTEN-FREE / NUT-FREE OPTION / SOY-FREE OPTION

These fritters are full of flavor and healthier than most fritters because they're baked, not fried. They're still decadent, especially when drizzled with ranch dressing.

Nonstick cooking spray

2 tablespoons chia seeds

6 tablespoons water

6 cups cauliflower rice (about
  2 large heads)

1 cup shredded vegan Cheddar cheese

1½ teaspoons chili powder

1 teaspoon dried parsley

1 teaspoon onion powder

1 teaspoon garlic powder

½ teaspoon salt

¼ teaspoon black pepper

⅛ teaspoon red pepper flakes

Vegan ranch dressing, for topping

1. Preheat the oven to 400°F. Lightly mist 12 cups of a muffin tin with cooking spray.

2. In a small bowl, make a "chia egg" by whisking the chia seeds with the water. Set aside.

3. Using paper towels, squeeze out the moisture from the cauliflower rice. Add the cauliflower to a large bowl. Stir in the chia egg, cheese, chili powder, parsley, onion powder, garlic powder, salt, black pepper, and red pepper flakes until well combined.

4. Spoon the cauliflower mixture into the muffin tin cups, filling each about three-quarters full.

5. Bake for 20 to 25 minutes, until a light golden brown. Let the fritters cool for a few minutes before plating, then drizzle with ranch dressing. Serve with additional dressing on the side for dipping.

VARIATION: Whip up half a batch of Super Smoky Seitan Bacon (page 149), then chop it and add it to the fritter mixture before baking.

DIY: Make your own ranch dressing (page 145).

SPICY GUACAMOLE

SERVES 6 / PREP TIME: 20 minutes, plus up to 1 hour to chill
GLUTEN-FREE OPTION / NUT-FREE OPTION / SOY-FREE OPTION

Avocados are sometimes called "nature's sour cream," and that's true even when they're used in spicy guacamole. If you'd like a little less heat, start with just one jalapeño or serrano. Enjoy this version with chips or atop Chick'n Fajitas (page 78), and don't forget to wear gloves when cutting the chiles!

3 avocados, halved, peeled, and pitted (pits reserved)

2 Roma (plum) tomatoes, diced, seeds and juice discarded

½ red onion, diced

2 jalapeño peppers or 1 jalapeño and 1 serrano pepper, seeded and diced

1 teaspoon minced garlic

3 tablespoons lime juice

½ teaspoon salt

½ teaspoon ground cumin

½ cup chopped fresh cilantro (optional)

Diced vegan bacon, for topping

1. Put the avocados in a large bowl and smash with the back of a fork. Add the tomatoes, onion, jalapeños, garlic, lime juice, salt, cumin, and cilantro (if using). Stir well to combine.

2. Return the avocado pits to the bowl. Cover the guacamole with a layer of plastic wrap, pushing it down carefully so there is no air between the guac and the plastic. Add a second layer of plastic wrap over the top of the bowl. Refrigerate for 30 to 60 minutes to allow the flavors to meld.

3. Remove the avocado pits (if you will have leftovers, save the pits and repeat the double-layer of plastic wrap to store). Sprinkle the bacon over the top and serve.

VARIATION: Want to make it even hotter? Try keeping in some of the chiles' ribs—that's where a pepper's heat lives.

DIY: Make your own bacon (page 149).

JALAPEÑO POPPERS

SERVES 6 / PREP TIME: 20 minutes **/ COOK TIME:** 20 minutes
NUT-FREE OPTION / SOY-FREE OPTION

Showing up to a potluck or picnic with these poppers is guaranteed to make you popular. Be sure to wear gloves when slicing the jalapeños.

8 ounces vegan cream cheese

1 cup shredded vegan Cheddar cheese

3 tablespoons thinly sliced scallions

½ teaspoon garlic powder

1 tablespoon vegan butter, melted

¼ cup panko bread crumbs

½ teaspoon salt

12 jalapeño peppers, halved lengthwise and seeded

1. Preheat the oven to 400°F.

2. In a bowl, combine the cream cheese, Cheddar, scallions, and garlic powder and mix well.

3. In a separate small bowl, stir together the melted butter, panko, and salt.

4. Spoon the cream cheese mixture into the jalapeño halves, then top with the panko mixture. Arrange in a single layer in a baking dish and bake for 20 minutes, or until the tops are golden brown. Let the poppers cool slightly before serving.

VARIATION: You can substitute gluten-free panko bread crumbs to make these poppers allergen-friendly!

DIY: Make your own cream cheese (page 138) and butter (page 146).

CHICK'N FINGERS

SERVES 4 / PREP TIME: 20 minutes / **COOK TIME:** 40 minutes
NUT-FREE OPTION / SOY-FREE OPTION

These fingers are perfect for a fun pick-me-up snack. Serve them with ketchup, barbecue sauce, or Zesty Vegan Ranch Dressing (page 145) for dipping. They're also delicious chopped on top of a salad.

Nonstick cooking spray

1 cup panko bread crumbs

2 tablespoons vegetable oil

2 teaspoons Italian seasoning

½ teaspoon salt (omit if the Italian seasoning has salt)

¼ teaspoon black pepper

1 cup unsweetened nondairy milk

½ cup cornstarch

2 loaves Mouthwatering Seitan "Meat" (page 147)

1. Preheat the oven to 375°F and move the oven rack to the lowest position. Lightly mist a rimmed baking sheet with cooking spray.

2. Set up three dredging bowls: In one bowl, combine the panko, oil, Italian seasoning, salt (if using), and pepper. Add the milk to a second bowl and the cornstarch to a third bowl.

3. Cut the seitan into "fingers." Dip each finger first into the cornstarch, then the milk, then the cornstarch again, and then the milk again. Roll it in the panko mixture until evenly coated. Place all the seitan fingers on the prepared baking sheet in a single layer.

4. Spritz the tops with cooking spray and bake on the bottom rack for 30 to 40 minutes, until they're golden brown. Flip them once halfway through and spritz the tops again with cooking spray. Serve warm.

MAKE AHEAD: Make the seitan ahead of time and store refrigerated in an airtight container for up to 5 days.

DIY: Make your own milk (page 140).

SOUTHERN SKILLET CORN · 44

CHAPTER FOUR

ALL-STAR SIDES

. . . .

GARLIC BUTTER SPINACH

SERVES 4 / PREP TIME: 1 minute / **COOK TIME:** 6 minutes
GLUTEN-FREE / NUT-FREE OPTION / SOY-FREE OPTION

This side dish will turn anyone into a fan of spinach. It's rich, buttery, and garlicky, with just a hint of lemon. It goes well with pretty much any meal.

2 tablespoons vegan butter

1 teaspoon minced garlic

1 pound baby spinach

½ teaspoon lemon juice

½ teaspoon salt

¼ teaspoon black pepper

1. In a large skillet, melt the butter over medium heat. Add the garlic and sauté for 1 to 2 minutes, stirring frequently.

2. Pile the spinach atop the garlic and continue to stir frequently as the spinach wilts, 2 to 3 minutes. Remove the pan from the heat and stir in the lemon juice, salt, and pepper. Taste and add more seasoning as desired.

VARIATION: Sprinkle on some red pepper flakes before serving to give the spinach extra bite!

DIY: Make your own butter (page 146).

LEMON-BASIL CAULIFLOWER RICE

SERVES 4 / PREP TIME: 5 minutes / **COOK TIME:** 8 minutes
GLUTEN-FREE / NUT-FREE OPTION / SOY-FREE OPTION

Rich, buttery rice is a staple in many comforting meals. This rice makes an especially great side dish for meals that are light on veggies.

3 cups cauliflower rice (about
 1 large head)
2 tablespoons vegan butter

½ teaspoon salt
Juice of 1 small lemon
18 to 20 basil leaves

1. Gently squeeze the cauliflower rice in a clean towel to remove any excess liquid.

2. Heat a saucepan over medium-high heat. Melt the butter, then add the cauliflower rice. Stir, then cover and cook for 5 to 6 minutes, until the rice is tender.

3. Reduce the heat to low and stir in the salt. Then add the lemon juice, 1 teaspoon at a time, to taste.

4. Chiffonade the basil by stacking the leaves and then rolling them into a tube shape. Slice into thin ribbons, then stir into the rice and remove from the heat.

VARIATION: Instead of making your own cauliflower rice with a grater, use a 16-ounce bag of frozen cauliflower rice. Just microwave it per the package instructions and squeeze out the excess liquid.

DIY: Make your own butter (page 146).

SOUTHERN SKILLET CORN

SERVES 6 / PREP TIME: 5 minutes / **COOK TIME:** 15 minutes
GLUTEN-FREE / NUT-FREE OPTION / SOY-FREE OPTION

Southern cooking is known for being decadent, and this skillet corn is no exception. It's creamy and satisfying, and the salt brings out the corn's natural sweetness.

4 tablespoons vegan butter

2 cups sweet corn

¼ cup unsweetened nondairy milk

1 tablespoon sugar

½ teaspoon salt

¼ teaspoon black pepper

1 tablespoon cornstarch

¼ cup water

1. Heat a large skillet over medium-high heat. Melt the butter and stir in the corn, milk, sugar, salt, and pepper. Reduce the heat to low, cover, and simmer for 10 minutes, stirring occasionally.

2. Meanwhile, in a small bowl, whisk together the cornstarch and water.

3. Once the corn has cooked for 10 minutes, stir in the cornstarch slurry and cook, uncovered, for another 5 minutes, stirring frequently. Add more salt and pepper to taste. Serve warm.

VARIATION: It may not be authentic, but I enjoy adding ½ tablespoon sweet paprika along with the other seasonings in step 1. Smoked paprika would be great, too!

DIY: Make your own butter (page 146) and milk (page 140).

BACON-RANCH PASTA SALAD

SERVES 4 / PREP TIME: 15 minutes, plus 1 hour to chill / **COOK TIME:** 10 minutes
NUT-FREE OPTION / SOY-FREE OPTION

I've made a lot (a real lot!) of pasta salads over the years, and this one is hands-down my favorite. There's just something about the flavorful ranch seasonings mixed with the tangy mayo and smoky seitan bacon.

½ (16-ounce) box pasta, such as rotini or similar size

1¼ cups vegan mayonnaise

¼ cup unsweetened nondairy milk

2 teaspoons dried parsley

1 teaspoon dried dill

1 teaspoon onion powder

1 teaspoon garlic powder

½ teaspoon salt

½ teaspoon black pepper

20 grape tomatoes, halved lengthwise

6 to 8 slices vegan bacon, cut crosswise into thin strips

1 (2.25-ounce) can sliced black olives, drained

2 or 3 scallions, thinly sliced (optional)

1. Cook the pasta to al dente according to the package directions. Rinse well with cold water.

2. In a large bowl, whisk together the mayonnaise and milk. Stir in the parsley, dill, onion powder, garlic powder, salt, and pepper. Stir in the tomatoes, bacon, and olives. Taste and add additional seasoning as desired.

3. Stir in the cooled pasta, cover, and refrigerate for at least 1 hour before serving. Top with the scallions, if desired.

MAKE AHEAD: This pasta salad will stay fresh refrigerated in an airtight container for up to 4 days. However, you might want to stir in ¼ cup additional vegan mayo before serving.

DIY: Make your own mayo (page 139), milk (page 140), and bacon (page 149).

CORN BREAD

SERVES 8 / PREP TIME: 10 minutes / **COOK TIME:** 22 minutes
NUT-FREE OPTION / SOY-FREE OPTION

Sweet, crumbly corn bread—whether you're serving it alongside your favorite soup or as a snack drizzled with maple syrup, it always hits the spot. Try it with the Green Chile Stew (page 68) or the Butternut Squash and Black Bean Stew (page 56).

Nonstick cooking spray
1 cup all-purpose flour
¼ cup cornmeal
⅓ cup packed light brown sugar
1 tablespoon baking powder
½ teaspoon salt

4 tablespoons vegan butter, melted
1 cup unsweetened nondairy milk
3 tablespoons real maple syrup,
  plus more for serving (optional)
Vegan butter, for serving (optional)

1. Preheat the oven to 400°F. Lightly mist an 8-inch square baking pan with cooking spray and set aside.

2. In a large bowl, combine the flour, cornmeal, brown sugar, baking powder, and salt.

3. In a medium bowl, combine the melted butter, milk, and maple syrup and stir until just combined. Pour the milk mixture into the flour mixture and stir just until combined.

4. Scrape the batter into the baking pan and bake for 20 to 22 minutes, until a toothpick inserted into the center comes out clean. Let cool in the pan on a wire rack for 5 to 10 minutes before serving with butter and maple syrup (if desired).

VARIATION: To add a little spice, drain a 4-ounce can of roasted green chiles and add it to the mixture in step 3. A fresh jalapeno, chopped or sliced into rounds would be delicious!

DIY: Make your own milk (page 140) and butter (page 146).

BACON-ROASTED BRUSSELS SPROUTS

SERVES 4 / PREP TIME: 15 minutes / **COOK TIME:** 40 minutes
GLUTEN-FREE OPTION / NUT-FREE OPTION / SOY-FREE OPTION

I know a lot of people who grew up believing the only way to eat Brussels sprouts was oven-roasted with bacon. I never tried that, but I sure am a fan of the vegan version!

1 pound Brussels sprouts, trimmed

3 tablespoons avocado or olive oil

½ teaspoon salt

½ teaspoon smoked paprika

½ teaspoon garlic powder

¼ teaspoon black pepper

6 slices vegan bacon, cut crosswise
   into strips

1. Preheat the oven to 400°F. Line a rimmed baking sheet with parchment paper.

2. In a bowl, toss the Brussels sprouts with the oil, salt, smoked paprika, garlic powder, and pepper. Spread evenly onto the prepared baking sheet and bake for 30 minutes, stirring once about halfway through.

3. Remove the baking sheet from the oven and stir in the sliced bacon. Return to the oven and bake for another 5 to 10 minutes, until the sprouts are crisp on the outside and tender on the inside.

VARIATION: Frozen Brussels sprouts will work for this recipe, but they will be softer and less crispy. If using frozen sprouts, do not thaw them. Bake them for 15 minutes, then toss with the oil and seasonings, stir in the bacon, and bake for another 10 minutes.

DIY: Make your own bacon (page 149).

LOADED BAKED POTATO CASSEROLE

SERVES 6 / **PREP TIME:** 10 minutes / **COOK TIME:** 45 minutes

GLUTEN-FREE OPTION / **NUT-FREE OPTION** / **SOY-FREE OPTION**

Baked potatoes are the perfect vehicle for whatever flavors you're craving, but my favorite is the classic loaded version. This casserole combines vegan bacon, cheese, and sour cream to create a truly comforting side dish . . . or meal.

2¾ pounds russet or red potatoes, well scrubbed

4 tablespoons vegan butter

½ cup unsweetened nondairy milk

1 cup vegan sour cream

5 scallions, sliced, divided

2 cups shredded vegan Cheddar cheese, divided

12 slices vegan bacon, cut crosswise into thin slices, divided

1 teaspoon salt

¼ teaspoon black pepper

1. Preheat the oven to 350°F.

2. Peel about half the potatoes and cut them all into cubes. Bring a large pot of water to a boil over medium-high heat, add the potatoes, and boil for 15 to 20 minutes, until tender.

3. Drain the potatoes and transfer to a large bowl. Mash to your desired consistency, then stir in the butter, milk, sour cream, about three-quarters of the sliced scallions, 1½ cups of cheese, the sliced bacon, the salt, and the pepper. Add an additional tablespoon of milk if the mixture is too dry; you want it to be slightly more liquid than you would serve as mashed potatoes, because it will firm up in the oven.

4. Scoop the mixture into a 2-quart baking dish and sprinkle evenly with the remaining scallions and remaining ½ cup of cheese. Bake for 25 minutes, or until the cheese is melted and the potatoes are heated through.

MAKE AHEAD: The potatoes can be prepped and boiled the night before to save time. Preheat the oven and proceed as directed in step 3. Keep in mind that because they're cold, they may need an extra 5 to 10 minutes in the oven.

DIY: Make your own butter (page 146), milk (page 140), sour cream (page 136), and bacon (page 149).

RANCH MASHED CAULIFLOWER

SERVES 4 / PREP TIME: 10 minutes / **COOK TIME:** 20 minutes
GLUTEN-FREE / NUT-FREE OPTION / SOY-FREE OPTION

Substituting cauliflower for potatoes is a great way to boost the nutrients in your mash. This ranch-flavored cauliflower is like a dinner version of chips and dip. Who's going to say no to that?

1 large head cauliflower, cut into florets
2 tablespoons vegan butter, at room
   temperature
¼ cup unsweetened nondairy milk
⅓ to ½ cup vegan ranch dressing

½ teaspoon salt
¼ teaspoon black pepper
Chopped fresh parsley, for garnish
   (optional)

1. Bring a medium saucepan of water to a boil over medium-high heat. Add the cauliflower and cook for 10 minutes, or until tender.

2. Drain the cauliflower and transfer to a food processor along with the butter and milk. Pulse until smooth.

3. Return the cauliflower mixture to the pan and place over low heat. Stir in the ranch, salt, and pepper and heat through. Taste and add more ranch dressing or salt as needed. Serve warm, garnished with parsley, if desired.

LIGHTEN UP: You can skip the butter and add an extra 2 tablespoons milk.

DIY: Make your own butter (page 146), milk (page 140), and ranch dressing (page 145).

COCONUT CURRY NOODLE SOUP · 66

CHAPTER FIVE

SOOTHING SOUPS

. . . .

BUTTERNUT SQUASH AND BLACK BEAN STEW

SERVES 4 / **PREP TIME:** 5 minutes / **COOK TIME:** 15 minutes

GLUTEN-FREE / NUT-FREE / SOY-FREE

Don't let the simplicity of this stew fool you—it is full of flavor. The savory butternut squash and smoked paprika are a wonderful combination. I recommend a topping of fresh basil or parsley and a side of hot buttered bread.

2 cups vegetable broth

1 (10-ounce) bag frozen butternut
   squash cubes

1 cup frozen sweet corn

1 (15.5-ounce) can black beans, drained
   and rinsed

1 (10.75-ounce) can tomato puree

1 teaspoon ground cumin

1 teaspoon dried oregano

½ teaspoon garlic powder

½ teaspoon onion powder

½ teaspoon smoked paprika

½ teaspoon salt

¼ teaspoon black pepper

Fresh herbs, for topping (optional)

1. In a large pot, bring the broth to a boil. Stir in the butternut squash and corn and return to a boil. Reduce the heat to medium-low.

2. Stir in the beans, tomato puree, cumin, oregano, garlic powder, onion powder, paprika, salt, and pepper and simmer uncovered, stirring occasionally, for 8 to 10 minutes. Top with fresh herbs before serving, if desired.

MAKE AHEAD: This stew makes for excellent leftovers, as a day or two in the fridge gives the flavors time to develop.

LASAGNA SOUP

SERVES 6 / PREP TIME: 10 minutes / **COOK TIME:** 15 minutes
NUT-FREE OPTION / SOY-FREE OPTION

This soup is a fun alternative to the classic pasta dish, and you can substitute any bite-size pasta you happen to have in the pantry. The soup becomes tastier after a day or two in the refrigerator.

1 tablespoon olive oil
1 onion, diced
1 zucchini, diced
1 carrot, sliced
1 tablespoon Italian seasoning
1 (14.5-ounce) can diced tomatoes, undrained
4 cups vegetable broth
⅓ cup jarred pasta sauce

2 bay leaves
½ (16-ounce) box lasagna noodles, broken into bite-size pieces, or small pasta of choice
½ teaspoon salt
¼ teaspoon black pepper
1 cup vegan ricotta cheese
1 cup shredded vegan mozzarella cheese
Fresh basil leaves (optional)

1. In a large saucepan, heat the oil over medium heat. Add the onion and sauté for 2 to 3 minutes, stirring frequently. Add the zucchini, carrot, and Italian seasoning and keep stirring for another minute or so.

2. Pour in the diced tomatoes and their juices, broth, and pasta sauce. Add the bay leaves and bring to a boil. Add the noodles, then reduce the heat and let simmer, covered, for about 10 minutes, or until the pasta is tender. Remove from the heat.

3. Remove the bay leaves and stir in the salt, pepper, ricotta, and about half of the mozzarella. Sprinkle the remaining mozzarella on the individual servings and top with basil, if desired.

VARIATION: Make this soup meaty by adding 1 loaf Mouthwatering Seitan "Meat" (page 147)! I recommend cutting up the seitan like chicken, not crumbling it. (If you're using store-bought, add 1 cup.)

DIY: Make your own ricotta (page 141).

BROCCOLI-CHEDDAR SOUP

SERVES 4 / PREP TIME: 10 minutes **/ COOK TIME:** 15 minutes
NUT-FREE OPTION / SOY-FREE OPTION

I thought I had said goodbye forever to this thick and creamy soup, but it turns out the vegan version is just as good as the original! It's the perfect combination of healthy (broccoli is a great source of calcium and vitamin K) and comforting, with all the gooey cheese.

4 tablespoons vegan butter

½ teaspoon onion powder

½ teaspoon garlic powder

¼ cup all-purpose flour

2 cups unsweetened nondairy milk, plus more as needed

1½ cups vegetable broth

4 cups small broccoli florets (about 1 head)

1 cup shredded vegan Cheddar cheese

½ cup shredded vegan Jack cheese

½ teaspoon salt

¼ teaspoon black pepper

Pinch ground nutmeg

1. In a saucepan, melt the butter over medium heat. Stir in the onion powder and garlic powder and let bubble for 1 minute. Add the flour, whisking until combined, and cook for 2 to 3 minutes.

2. Pour in the milk and broth and bring to a boil, stirring often so that the milk doesn't scald. Add the broccoli, then reduce the heat and simmer, covered, for 10 minutes, until thick.

3. Stir in both cheeses, the salt, pepper, and nutmeg. Simmer uncovered for another 2 minutes, or until the cheese has melted. If the soup is too thick, add an additional 2 to 3 tablespoons of milk, stirring until combined.

LIGHTEN UP: To save calories (and to make this gluten-free), skip the butter and flour roux, adding the onion powder and garlic powder with the other seasonings in step 3. Keep in mind that the soup won't be quite as thick.

DIY: Make your own butter (page 146) and milk (page 140).

CHICK'N NOODLE SOUP

SERVES 4 / **PREP TIME:** 10 minutes / **COOK TIME:** 20 minutes
NUT-FREE / **SOY-FREE OPTION**

This vegan version of the best-known comfort food is sure to please. Just the smell of it is enough to lift my spirits, and it's light enough to enjoy year-round.

1 tablespoon olive oil

1 small sweet onion, diced

½ teaspoon minced garlic

2 carrots, cut into ½-inch rounds

2 celery stalks, cut into ½-inch pieces

1 small sweet potato, peeled and cut into bite-size pieces

2 bay leaves

½ teaspoon dried thyme

½ teaspoon salt

¼ teaspoon black pepper

5 cups vegetable broth

½ (16-ounce) package fideo (cut spaghetti) pasta

1 cup chopped vegan chick'n (unbreaded) or Mouthwatering Seitan "Meat" (page 147)

1. In a large soup pot, heat the oil over medium heat. Add the onion and sauté for 2 to 3 minutes, stirring frequently. Add the garlic and sauté for another minute or so, still stirring frequently.

2. Add the carrots, celery, sweet potato, bay leaves, thyme, salt, pepper, and broth and bring to a boil. Reduce the heat and simmer uncovered for 10 minutes.

3. Add the pasta and simmer for another 5 to 6 minutes, until the pasta is al dente. Add some water if too much broth has evaporated. Stir in the chick'n and simmer for another minute or so until heated through. Serve warm.

LIGHTEN UP: Substitute canned chickpeas or cannellini beans for the chick'n.

TOMATO-BASIL SOUP

SERVES 4 / PREP TIME: 15 minutes / **COOK TIME:** 30 minutes
NUT-FREE OPTION / SOY-FREE OPTION

Tomatoes and basil go together perfectly, and this creamy soup is a great example of the delectable duo in action! Try serving it with buttered toast or your favorite grilled cheese sandwich.

4 tablespoons vegan butter

½ sweet onion, diced

½ teaspoon minced garlic

¼ cup all-purpose flour

1 (28-ounce) can crushed tomatoes

1 (8-ounce) can tomato sauce

4 cups vegetable broth

2 teaspoons sugar

1 teaspoon salt, plus more to taste

½ teaspoon black pepper, plus more to taste

18 to 20 fresh basil leaves, divided

1. In a medium saucepan, melt the butter over medium-high heat. Add the onion and sauté, stirring frequently, for 2 minutes. Add the garlic and cook, stirring frequently, for another 4 to 5 minutes, until both are soft.

2. Whisk in the flour and reduce the heat to medium. Cook, stirring, for another 3 to 4 minutes.

3. Add the tomatoes, tomato sauce, broth, sugar, salt, and pepper. Bring to a boil, reduce the heat to low, and simmer uncovered for 15 minutes.

4. Add about three-quarters of the basil leaves and cook for another 5 minutes. Remove from the heat.

〉〉

5. Use an immersion blender to puree the soup. (If using a regular blender, let the soup cool, then puree in small batches, and reheat it before serving.) Taste the soup and add more salt and pepper as desired. Chop the remaining basil leaves and serve the soup topped with the additional basil.

MAKE AHEAD: This soup reheats nicely for leftovers. I recommend stirring in a few tablespoons of your favorite unsweetened nondairy milk to keep the consistency smooth.

DIY: Make your own butter (page 146).

SPICY CHICK'N AND VEGGIE CHOWDER

SERVES 4 / **PREP TIME:** 15 minutes / **COOK TIME:** 25 minutes
NUT-FREE OPTION / SOY-FREE OPTION

I like this chowder spicy, so I'll sometimes add a second jalapeño pepper. The heat is in the ribs, so if you want it even hotter, be sure to leave those in!

2 to 3 tablespoons water
1 red bell pepper, diced
½ sweet onion, diced
1 jalapeño pepper, diced
4 tablespoons vegan butter
¼ cup all-purpose flour
2½ cups vegetable broth
2 cups unsweetened nondairy milk

2 red potatoes, cut into bite-size pieces
1 carrot, diced
2 cups sliced vegan chick'n (unbreaded)
    or Mouthwatering Seitan "Meat"
    (page 147)
1 teaspoon red pepper flakes
½ teaspoon salt
¼ teaspoon black pepper

1. In a medium saucepan, heat the water over medium-high heat. Add the bell pepper, onion, and jalapeño and water-sauté for 3 to 4 minutes. Remove the vegetables from the saucepan and set aside on a plate.

2. With the (now-empty) saucepan still over medium-high heat, melt the butter and whisk in the flour. Cook, stirring frequently, for 2 to 3 minutes.

3. Whisk in the broth and milk until smooth, then add the potatoes and carrots. Bring to a boil, then reduce the heat to low and simmer, uncovered, for 10 to 12 minutes, until the potatoes are tender.

4. Stir in the sautéed vegetables, the chick'n, red pepper flakes, salt, and black pepper. Let simmer for another 2 to 3 minutes. Taste and add more seasoning as desired.

   LIGHTEN UP: You can skip the vegan chick'n and double the veggies instead.
   DIY: Make your own butter (page 146) and milk (page 140).

BACON-POTATO CHOWDER

SERVES 4 / **PREP TIME:** 15 minutes / **COOK TIME:** 20 minutes
NUT-FREE OPTION / **SOY-FREE OPTION**

Growing up in New England basically makes me a "chowdah" expert, and I'm here to tell you this one is the best because it has bacon! This is a very stick-to-your-ribs chowder, perfect for a chilly day. It's like a hug for your tummy! It also makes great leftovers; just keep in mind you'll want to add a little extra milk to thin it out when reheating.

2 tablespoons vegan butter

½ sweet onion, diced

2 tablespoons all-purpose flour

3 cups vegetable broth

3 medium russet potatoes, peeled and
    cut into bite-size pieces

3 celery stalks, sliced

1 large carrot, diced

1 cup sweet corn

½ teaspoon salt, plus more to taste

¼ teaspoon black pepper

1 cup unsweetened nondairy milk,
    plus more as needed

12 slices vegan bacon, thinly sliced

1. In a soup pot, melt the butter over medium-high heat. Add the onion and sauté for 1 to 2 minutes.

2. Stir in the flour and cook for another 2 to 3 minutes, stirring frequently. Add the broth and whisk until the roux dissolves.

3. Add the potatoes, celery, and carrot. Increase the heat to high and bring to a boil, then reduce the heat to low and simmer, uncovered, for 10 to 12 minutes. When the potatoes are fork-tender, stir in the corn and remove the pot from the heat.

4. Put about half the chowder in a bowl and use an immersion blender to puree it before returning it to the pot. (If using a regular blender, let the soup cool, then puree in small batches.)

5. Return to medium-low heat and stir in the salt, pepper, milk, and bacon. Let simmer for 1 to 2 minutes, or until heated through. Add more milk as needed to achieve the desired consistency.

VARIATION: If you don't have a blender, it's fine to skip that step. The chowder will still be delicious, just a little less thick.

DIY: Make your own butter (page 146), milk (page 140), and bacon (page 149).

COCONUT CURRY NOODLE SOUP

SERVES 4 / PREP TIME: 15 minutes / **COOK TIME:** 25 minutes
NUT-FREE

"Curry" is an Anglicized term used to describe a wide variety of dishes, typically containing proteins or vegetables cooked in a spice-based sauce and often served over rice or noodles. There are many different varieties of what Anglophones call "curry" that have originated in many different countries. Each has its own unique spice mixture, sauce base, flavor, heat level, and even color. When given a choice, I always go for a coconut-based curry because I love the creaminess and hint of sweetness. This recipe is my own take on a curry that incorporates yellow curry powder and a coconut and veggie broth base. It's not spicy, so if you're a fiend for heat, try using red curry paste instead of the yellow curry powder.

1 tablespoon olive oil

½ small onion, thinly sliced

2 tablespoons yellow curry powder

½ teaspoon ground coriander

½ teaspoon ground ginger

½ teaspoon garlic powder

1 (13.5-ounce) can full-fat coconut milk, well shaken

3 cups vegetable broth

2 tablespoons soy sauce

1 cup chopped peeled sweet potato

1½ cups broccoli florets

1 red bell pepper, thinly sliced

5 ounces rice noodles

Lime wedges and bean sprouts, for serving (optional)

1. In a large soup pot, heat the oil over medium heat. Add the onion, curry powder, coriander, ginger, and garlic powder. Cook for 2 to 3 minutes, stirring frequently, until the seasonings "bloom" and their scent becomes wonderfully intense.

2. Add the coconut milk, broth, soy sauce, and sweet potato. Bring to a boil, then reduce the heat and simmer uncovered for 5 minutes.

3. Add the broccoli and bell pepper and simmer uncovered for another 10 to 15 minutes, until the veggies are tender.

4. While the curry and veggies are simmering, cook the rice noodles in a separate pot according to the package directions. Rinse in cold water and set aside.

5. Stir the noodles into the curry soup and continue to simmer for 1 to 2 minutes. Squeeze a lime over each serving, and top with a handful of bean sprouts, if desired.

MAKE AHEAD: If you want to make this soup ahead of time (or are planning to enjoy some of it as leftovers), keep the noodles separate until you're ready to serve.

GREEN CHILE STEW

SERVES 4 / PREP TIME: 20 minutes / **COOK TIME:** 25 minutes
GLUTEN-FREE / NUT-FREE / SOY-FREE

Since moving to Colorado, I've become a dedicated fan of green chiles! Hatch is the best-known variety (from Hatch, New Mexico, the "chile capitol of the world") and is known for its garlicky, sweet, spicy, and smoky flavor. As a Coloradan, I'm partial to Pueblo green chiles from Pueblo, Colorado, but they tend to be much hotter than the Hatch variety. You really can't go wrong with either one!

2 tablespoons vegetable oil

1 small onion, diced

1½ teaspoons minced garlic

2 teaspoons ground cumin

1 teaspoon dried oregano

½ teaspoon sweet paprika

½ teaspoon salt

¼ teaspoon black pepper

3 fire-roasted Hatch or Pueblo green
   chiles, skinned and diced

1 small zucchini, diced

1 (16-ounce) jar salsa verde

5 cups vegetable broth

1 cup sweet corn

½ cup long-grain white rice

Juice of 1 lime

Fresh cilantro, sliced avocado, and
   tortilla chips, for topping (optional)

1. In a large soup pot, heat the oil over medium-high heat. Add the onion and sauté for 2 to 3 minutes, stirring frequently. Add the garlic and cook for another 3 minutes.

2. Stir in the cumin, oregano, paprika, salt, and pepper and cook for another minute or so, until the seasonings "bloom" and become fragrant.

3. Increase the heat to high and add the chiles, zucchini, salsa verde, broth, corn, and rice. As soon as the mixture begins to boil, reduce the heat and simmer for 15 to 18 minutes, until the rice is tender.

4. Stir in the lime juice and serve with your desired toppings.

VARIATION: To make this more "authentic," stir in 2 cups shredded vegan chick'n in step 3. This will also increase the number of servings to six. Also, feel free to swap in 1 cup beer for 1 cup of the vegetable broth to add more flavor!

CHAPTER SIX

HEARTY HANDHELDS

· · · · · · · ·

BARBECUE VEGGIE GRILLED CHEESE

SERVES 4 / PREP TIME: 15 minutes / **COOK TIME:** 15 minutes
NUT-FREE OPTION / SOY-FREE OPTION

I love how each time I make this hearty, gooey grilled cheese it turns out a little bit different. Sometimes I use sourdough bread, sometimes I use a spicy barbecue sauce, and I love to switch it up with Cheddar and smoked Gouda. Play around and find your favorite combination!

2 tablespoons water

2½ cups sliced button or baby bella mushrooms

¾ cup barbecue sauce, divided

3 to 4 tablespoons vegan butter

8 thick slices hearty bread

2 to 2½ cups shredded vegan cheese

1. Heat a large skillet over medium-high heat. Add the water and mushrooms and water-sauté for 3 to 4 minutes.

2. Stir in ½ cup of barbecue sauce and reduce the heat to low. Stirring frequently, simmer for another 4 to 5 minutes, until the mushrooms are soft. Spoon the mushrooms and sauce into a bowl and wipe out the skillet.

3. Return the skillet to medium heat. Butter one side of each slice of bread and place 4 slices butter-side down in the pan. Layer on half of the cheese, 2 spoonfuls of the mushroom mixture, then more cheese, and a light drizzle of the remaining barbecue sauce. Top with the remaining slices of bread, butter-side up.

4. Cook for 2 to 3 minutes on each side, until the bread is crispy and golden-brown and the cheese is melted.

VARIATION: Instead of mushrooms, use slices of your favorite mock meat.
DIY: Make your own butter (page 146).

TACO BITES

SERVES 4 / **PREP TIME:** 15 minutes / **COOK TIME:** 20 minutes

NUT-FREE OPTION / SOY-FREE OPTION

These taco bites are easy to make and totally satisfying. Crescent rolls give them a rich, buttery flavor.

1 to 2 tablespoons vegetable oil

1 cup vegan "beef" crumbles or
   1 loaf Mouthwatering Seitan "Meat"
   (page 147), crumbled

2 tablespoons taco seasoning

3 tablespoons salsa

1 (8-count) tube refrigerated vegan
   crescent rolls

¾ cup shredded vegan Cheddar cheese
   (or a mix of cheddar and pepper jack)

Vegan sour cream, for dipping

1. Preheat the oven to 350°F.

2. Heat a skillet over medium-high heat. Add the oil to the pan, using 1 tablespoon for store-bought "beef" and 2 tablespoons for home-made seitan. Sauté for about 5 minutes, stirring frequently, or until the crumbles are browned and a little crispy. Add the taco season-ing and salsa and keep stirring for another 1 to 2 minutes. Remove from the heat.

3. Lay the crescent rolls out on a rimmed baking sheet. Place a pinch of cheese on the wide end, followed by a scoop of about 2 tablespoons of the taco "meat" onto each roll. Carefully roll the dough toward the thin end, so that the taco "meat" and cheese are covered.

4. Bake for 8 to 10 minutes, until the rolls are a light golden brown. Let cool for a few minutes before serving with sour cream for dipping.

VARIATION: Make 'em spicy! Add a diced jalapeño to the rolls along with the taco "meat," or add ½ teaspoon chili powder when adding the taco seasoning.

DIY: Make your own sour cream (page 136).

EGG-ISH SALAD SANDWICHES

SERVES 6 / PREP TIME: 15 minutes, plus 15 minutes to chill
NUT-FREE

Growing up, I loved egg salad sandwiches so much, but my mom rarely made them because it took so much time to boil, cool, and peel the eggs. This vegan version is much faster and just as yummy!

½ cup vegan mayonnaise

1 teaspoon garlic powder

½ teaspoon dried parsley

½ teaspoon onion powder

½ teaspoon kala namak

½ teaspoon sweet paprika

¼ teaspoon ground turmeric

¼ teaspoon black pepper

1 tablespoon yellow mustard

2 teaspoons spicy brown mustard

1 (14-ounce) package extra-firm tofu, well pressed

12 slices bread

Lettuce, tomato, and mustard, for topping (optional)

1. In a bowl, stir together the mayonnaise, garlic powder, parsley, onion powder, kala namak, paprika, turmeric, pepper, and both mustards.

2. Use your hands to crumble the tofu into little bits into the bowl. Stir well, cover, and refrigerate for at least 15 minutes to let the flavor soak into the tofu.

3. Make sandwiches on your favorite bread. Top with lettuce, tomato, and mustard, if desired.

MAKE AHEAD: Meal-prep a batch of this egg-ish salad and enjoy for lunch all week!

DIY: Make your own mayo (page 139).

FRENCH BREAD PIZZA

SERVES 4 / PREP TIME: 15 minutes / **COOK TIME:** 15 minutes
NUT-FREE OPTION / SOY-FREE OPTION

I ate a lot of pizza growing up, but French bread pizza was specific to weekends at my grandma's house. She served us the frozen kind, and I couldn't have cared less—it was always my number one request for dinner!

1 (16-ounce) loaf French bread
1 cup pizza sauce
2 cups shredded vegan
   mozzarella cheese

½ bell pepper, thinly sliced
½ sweet onion, thinly sliced
⅓ cup pitted, sliced green olives
½ teaspoon dried oregano

1. Preheat the oven to 400°F.

2. Slice the French bread in half horizontally and place both pieces on a rimmed baking sheet, cut-side up. Spread the pizza sauce evenly over both pieces of bread, using as much sauce as desired. Spread about three-quarters of the cheese over both pieces of bread. Add the bell pepper, onion, and green olives evenly across the top, then sprinkle on the remaining cheese and the oregano.

3. Bake for 12 to 15 minutes, rotating the baking sheet front to back halfway through, until the bread is crisp and the cheese is melted.

VARIATION: Substitute other veggies, such as black olives, mushrooms, and banana peppers, or even add some vegan pepperoni!

BUFFALO CHICK'N TAQUITOS

SERVES 6 / **PREP TIME:** 15 minutes / **COOK TIME:** 12 minutes

NUT-FREE OPTION / **SOY-FREE OPTION**

Buffalo sauce and chick'n (yes, even the vegan kind!) go together like best friends. These taquitos make a great snack, or pair them with some spicy rice and a fresh salad and suddenly they're a meal!

Nonstick cooking spray

4 ounces vegan cream cheese, at room temperature

⅓ cup vegan blue cheese dressing or vegan ranch dressing, plus more for dipping

¼ cup plus 2 tablespoons Buffalo sauce

3 scallions, thinly sliced

2 cups shredded vegan chick'n or Mouthwatering Seitan "Meat" (page 147)

1 cup shredded vegan cheddar cheese or a mix of cheddar and pepper jack (optional)

12 fajita-size flour tortillas

1. Preheat the oven to 415°F. Lightly mist a rimmed baking sheet with cooking spray.

2. In a medium bowl, whisk together the cream cheese, dressing, and Buffalo sauce. It's okay if there are still some tiny pieces of cream cheese. Stir in the scallions, chick'n, and shredded cheese (if using).

3. Using a soup spoon, scoop 2 spoonfuls of filling onto each tortilla, arranged along one edge. Starting with the edge that has the filling, roll up the tortilla tightly enough that the filling is near the openings at either end, but not so tightly that it spills out.

4. Lay the taquitos seam-side down on the prepared baking sheet, close to each other but not touching. Spritz the tops with cooking spray.

5. Bake for 10 to 12 minutes, until the edges of the tortillas are light brown and the whole taquito feels crispy. Let cool for a few minutes before serving with more ranch dressing for dipping.

MAKE AHEAD: The filling can be made the day before and refrigerated, but the taquitos are best when freshly baked. If you have leftovers to reheat, use an oven, toaster oven, or air fryer rather than a microwave.

DIY: Make your own cream cheese (page 138) and ranch dressing (page 145).

CHICK'N FAJITAS

SERVES 4 / PREP TIME: 15 minutes **/ COOK TIME:** 15 minutes
NUT-FREE OPTION / SOY-FREE OPTION

You know those big sizzling platters of fajitas you can get at Mexican restaurants? This is like that, but with about 100 times the veggies! Plus, since you're the chef, you can substitute your favorite vegetables and toppings and make it as spicy as you'd like.

About ½ cup water, divided

2 bell peppers, any color, cut into thin strips

1 small sweet onion, cut into thin strips

1 cup sliced button or baby bella mushrooms

1 tablespoon vegetable oil

1 cup sliced vegan chick'n or Mouthwatering Seitan "Meat" (page 147)

½ teaspoon sweet paprika

½ teaspoon dried oregano

½ teaspoon garlic powder

½ teaspoon salt

½ teaspoon ground cumin

¼ teaspoon chili powder

¼ teaspoon black pepper

¼ teaspoon red pepper flakes (optional)

1 teaspoon lime juice

8 fajita-size flour tortillas

Sliced avocado, vegan sour cream, and shredded vegan cheese, for topping (optional)

1. Heat a skillet over medium-high heat. Add 2 tablespoons of water, the bell peppers, onion, and mushrooms and water-sauté for 6 to 7 minutes, adding more water as necessary and stirring frequently, until the veggies are barely tender. Remove from the pan and set aside.

2. In the same pan, heat the oil. Add the chick'n strips and cook over medium heat for 5 minutes, stirring occasionally, until the pieces are lightly browned and slightly crispy on both sides.

3. Return the veggies to the pan. Add the paprika, oregano, garlic powder, salt, cumin, chili powder, black pepper, red pepper flakes (if using), and remaining ¼ cup plus 2 tablespoons of water. Reduce the heat to low and simmer until the water is almost gone. Add more water if you want a saucier filling. Stir in the lime juice. Serve in tortillas with your desired toppings.

LIGHTEN UP: Save calories and increase the vitamins by skipping the chick'n (and oil) and substituting 1 cup sliced zucchini. Simply cook the zucchini with the other vegetables in step 1 and skip step 2.

DIY: Make your own sour cream (page 136).

VEGGIE PITAS WITH TZATZIKI SAUCE

SERVES 4 / PREP TIME: 20 minutes
NUT-FREE OPTION

I love the bright, tangy flavor of this sauce, and it's also great as a dip. If you want to bulk up these sandwiches, try adding warm chickpeas!

FOR THE SAUCE

1 medium cucumber

1 (14-ounce) package firm tofu, drained but not pressed

½ cup unsweetened nondairy milk

2 teaspoons dried dill

1 to 1½ teaspoons minced garlic

1½ teaspoons apple cider vinegar

1½ teaspoons lemon juice

½ teaspoon salt

FOR THE PITAS

1 tomato, sliced

½ cucumber, sliced

1 large carrot, grated

4 small pitas or 2 large pitas, halved

½ teaspoon sweet paprika

Salt

Black pepper

1. Grate the cucumber and use a kitchen towel or paper towels to squeeze out as much liquid as possible.

2. In a blender or food processor, combine the tofu, milk, dill, garlic, vinegar, lemon juice, and salt and blend until completely smooth. Add the cucumber and pulse just once or twice. Cover and refrigerate the tzatziki sauce until ready to use.

3. Layer the veggies in the pitas and sprinkle with the paprika, salt, and pepper. Top generously with tzatziki sauce and enjoy.

   MAKE AHEAD: The tzatziki sauce will keep for up to 4 days when covered tightly and refrigerated.

   DIY: Make your own milk (page 140).

CHAPTER SEVEN

NOODLES FOR DAYS

· · · · · · · ·

FETTUCCINE ALFREDO WITH ROASTED VEGETABLES

SERVES 4 / **PREP TIME:** 10 minutes / **COOK TIME:** 20 minutes
NUT-FREE OPTION / **SOY-FREE OPTION**

Smooth, creamy Alfredo sauce is one of my favorite things. I went so many years without it when I first went vegan, and now I eat it two or three times a month (I'm making up for lost time)! You can skip the smoked paprika, but it does add a nice, light smoky taste to the veggies.

1 medium zucchini, finely chopped

1 red bell pepper, finely chopped

3 tablespoons olive oil

¼ teaspoon salt, plus more to taste

¼ teaspoon black pepper, plus more
   to taste

⅛ teaspoon smoked paprika (optional)

½ (16-ounce) box fettuccine pasta

1½ cups vegan Alfredo sauce

1. Preheat the oven to 400°F.

2. In a small bowl, toss the zucchini and bell pepper in the olive oil, salt, pepper, and smoked paprika (if using). Spread in a single layer on a rimmed baking sheet and bake for 15 to 20 minutes, stirring once, until they're soft and lightly charred.

3. Cook the pasta to al dente according to the package directions. Drain and return to the pot. Stir in the Alfredo sauce. Taste and add more salt and pepper if desired. Serve topped with the roasted veggies.

VARIATION: Instead of smoked paprika, add ¼ teaspoon cayenne pepper to the vegetables before roasting to add some heat.

DIY: Make your own Alfredo sauce (page 142).

CREAMY PENNE ALLA VODKA

SERVES 6 / PREP TIME: 10 minutes / **COOK TIME:** 25 minutes
NUT-FREE OPTION / SOY-FREE OPTION

This grown-up version of pasta is guaranteed to impress! If you're cooking on a gas stove, remove the pan from the heat before pouring in the alcohol. Don't skip the cream cheese—it makes it extra delectable!

1 (16-ounce) box penne pasta

3 tablespoons vegan butter

1 teaspoon minced garlic

½ cup vodka

1 (15-ounce) jar tomato sauce

1 cup unsweetened nondairy milk
(cashew or soy preferred)

¼ cup vegan cream cheese (optional)

¼ cup nutritional yeast, plus more for
topping (optional)

¼ to ½ teaspoon salt

¼ teaspoon red pepper flakes

⅛ teaspoon black pepper

Fresh basil, for topping (optional)

1. Cook the pasta to al dente according to the package directions. Drain and set aside.

2. Meanwhile, in a saucepan, melt the butter over medium-high heat. Stir in the garlic and cook for 2 minutes, stirring frequently. Stir in the vodka and cook for another 2 minutes.

3. Reduce the heat to low and add the tomato sauce, milk, cream cheese (if using), nutritional yeast, salt, red pepper flakes, and black pepper. Stir well and let sit over low heat until heated all the way through, 3 to 4 minutes.

4. Taste and add more salt or red pepper flakes as desired. Add the drained pasta to the pan. Stir well and serve topped with additional nutritional yeast or basil, if desired.

MAKE AHEAD: Reheated pasta can dry out, so try adding a couple tablespoons of nondairy milk or vegan butter when reheating.

DIY: Make your own butter (page 146), milk (page 140), and cream cheese (page 138).

RAMEN NOODLE STIR-FRY

SERVES 4 / PREP TIME: 10 minutes **/ COOK TIME:** 15 minutes
NUT-FREE

Ramen restaurants are popular, and here's an easy-yet-delicious version you can make at home. There are quite a few brands of vegan ramen out there, but for this recipe you can use any kind, because you're only using the noodles, not the seasoning packet (which is what may make it nonvegan). For extra flavor, try using sesame or chili oil for sautéing the veggies!

2 (3.5-ounce) packages instant
  ramen noodles

1 tablespoon vegetable oil

½ sweet onion, diced

½ teaspoon minced garlic

1½ cups broccoli florets

½ cup sliced water chestnuts

1½ cups sugar snap peas

½ cup vegetable broth

¼ cup soy sauce

3 tablespoons hoisin sauce

1 tablespoon rice vinegar

1 to 2 teaspoons sriracha

½ teaspoon ground ginger

2 or 3 scallions, thinly sliced

½ teaspoon toasted sesame seeds
  (optional)

1. Cook the noodles according to the package directions, but without the seasoning packet. Rinse with cold water and set aside.

2. Meanwhile, in a large skillet, heat the oil over medium-high heat until hot. Add the onion and sauté, stirring frequently, for 2 to 3 minutes. Add the garlic and cook for 1 more minute.

3. Stir in the broccoli, water chestnuts, and sugar snap peas. Stir in the broth, soy sauce, hoisin, vinegar, sriracha, and ginger. Reduce the heat, cover, and simmer for 6 to 7 minutes, until the vegetables are tender.

4. Uncover, stir in the noodles, and cook for another 1 to 2 minutes, until the noodles are hot. If the stir-fry gets too dry, add 1 to 2 tablespoons of soy sauce or water and stir well. Serve topped with the scallions and sesame seeds (if using).

VARIATION: Make it meaty! Add ½ cup thinly chopped seitan with the noodles in step 4. You may need to let the dish cook for an extra minute or so to warm the seitan through.

VEGETABLE LO MEIN

SERVES 4 / PREP TIME: 10 minutes / **COOK TIME:** 15 minutes

NUT-FREE

This lo mein is admittedly not traditional, but because most lo mein noodles are made with egg, I like to use regular spaghetti. If you'd prefer, you could also use any sort of rice noodle you have in your pantry.

½ (16-ounce) box spaghetti pasta

¼ cup soy sauce

1 teaspoon light brown sugar

2 teaspoons hoisin sauce

1 teaspoon toasted sesame oil

½ teaspoon ground ginger

½ teaspoon sriracha

2 to 3 tablespoons water

½ sweet onion, thinly sliced

½ teaspoon minced garlic

1 bell pepper, any color, thinly sliced

2 cups sliced button or baby bella mushrooms

2 cups spinach

1 cup sugar snap peas

1. Cook the pasta to al dente according to the package directions. Drain and set aside.

2. Meanwhile, in a small bowl, whisk together the soy sauce, brown sugar, hoisin, sesame oil, ginger, and sriracha. Set the sauce aside.

3. In a large skillet, heat the water over medium-high heat. Add the onion and water-sauté, stirring frequently, for 3 to 4 minutes, adding more water if the pan starts to dry out. Add the garlic and cook for 1 minute.

4. Add the bell pepper and mushrooms and cook, stirring frequently, for another 3 to 4 minutes. Finally, add the spinach and sugar snap peas and cook just until the spinach is wilted.

5. Reduce the heat to low and add the pasta and reserved sauce, stirring well to combine. Let heat through for 2 to 3 minutes. Serve.

VARIATION: Replace half or all the mushrooms with your favorite mock meat.

DECONSTRUCTED LASAGNA

SERVES 6 / **PREP TIME:** 15 minutes / **COOK TIME:** 30 minutes
NUT-FREE OPTION / **SOY-FREE OPTION**

Most lasagna recipes are a lot of work, but not this one. This deconstructed version lets you skip all the layering but still delivers the hot, saucy, gooey flavors we all love! This is my go-to recipe after a hard day when I need a really comforting meal.

2 cups water, divided

1 cup frozen diced bell peppers

½ cup frozen diced onion

½ teaspoon garlic powder

2 links vegan Italian sausage, cut into thin rounds

1 (24-ounce) jar pasta sauce

6 ounces lasagna noodles, broken into rough bite-size pieces

1½ cups shredded vegan mozzarella cheese, divided

1½ cups vegan ricotta cheese

Salt

Black pepper

Fresh basil leaves

1. Preheat the oven to 350°F.

2. In a Dutch oven or other ovenproof pot, heat ½ cup of water over medium heat. Add the bell peppers, onion, and garlic powder and water-sauté for 3 to 4 minutes. Stir in the remaining 1½ cups of water, the sliced sausage, and pasta sauce. Stir in the noodles and ½ cup of mozzarella.

3. Make sure the noodle pieces are lying flat in the pot, then spoon on the ricotta and top with the remaining 1 cup of mozzarella. Bake uncovered for 20 to 25 minutes, until the cheese is melted and the sauce is bubbling around the edges. Let sit for 5 minutes before serving. Sprinkle with salt and pepper to taste and some basil.

LIGHTEN UP: Skip the vegan sausage and substitute with 1 cup of your favorite veggies, like sliced mushrooms or diced squash.

DIY: Make your own ricotta (page 141).

CREAMY CAJUN PASTA

SERVES 4 / PREP TIME: 15 minutes / **COOK TIME:** 35 minutes
NUT-FREE OPTION

I love the combination of chewy, baked tofu and creamy pasta. You can buy premixed blackening seasoning at the store, but I like to make my own because I can add a little extra heat! Even if you don't go spicy, I think you'll love the deep, savory fragrance the spices add to the tofu.

Nonstick cooking spray

1 (14-ounce) package firm tofu, well pressed and cut into bite-size cubes

2 teaspoons vegetable oil

2 teaspoons sweet paprika

1 teaspoon dried thyme

½ teaspoon onion powder

½ teaspoon garlic powder

½ teaspoon dried oregano

½ teaspoon cayenne pepper

¼ teaspoon salt

¼ teaspoon black pepper

½ (16-ounce) box pasta, any shape

2 to 3 tablespoons water

¾ cup halved grape tomatoes

1½ cups vegan Alfredo sauce

Fresh parsley or basil (optional)

1. Preheat the oven to 375°F. Lightly mist a rimmed baking sheet with cooking spray.

2. In a medium bowl, combine the tofu, oil, paprika, thyme, onion powder, garlic powder, oregano, cayenne, salt, and black pepper and toss to coat.

3. Spread the tofu out on the prepared baking sheet in a single layer and bake for 25 to 30 minutes, flipping once, until lightly browned.

4. Meanwhile, cook the pasta to al dente according to the package directions. Drain and set aside.

5. Return the pasta pot to medium-high heat. Add the water and water-sauté the tomatoes until soft, 4 to 5 minutes. Add the Alfredo sauce and the drained pasta, reduce the heat to low, and cook for 2 to 3 minutes to warm through. Serve topped with the tofu and fresh herbs, if desired.

MAKE AHEAD: The tofu can be baked ahead of time and refrigerated in an airtight container for up to 3 days, until you're ready to serve.

DIY: Make your own Alfredo sauce (page 142).

DRUNKEN NOODLES

SERVES 4 / **PREP TIME:** 15 minutes / **COOK TIME:** 15 minutes
NUT-FREE

Many Thai restaurants offer this dish, but it is very rarely vegan even if it is meat-free. My version isn't authentic by any means, but it is made without fish or oyster sauce so that those who don't eat meat can partake.

1 (8-ounce) package rice noodles

¼ cup soy sauce

3 tablespoons hoisin sauce

1 to 2 tablespoons sriracha

2 tablespoons light brown sugar

1 tablespoon water

½ teaspoon ground ginger

1 tablespoon vegetable oil

¼ cup diced onion

1 teaspoon minced garlic

1 bell pepper, any color, cut into thin slices 2 inches long

1 carrot, julienned

1 cup chopped yellow squash

¼ cup sliced scallions

Fresh Thai or sweet basil, for garnish (optional)

Lime wedges, for serving (optional)

1. Cook the noodles according to the package directions. Drain, rinse with cold water, and set aside.

2. Meanwhile, in a small bowl, whisk together the soy sauce, hoisin, sriracha, brown sugar, water, and ginger. Set the sauce aside.

3. In a large saucepan, heat the oil over medium heat. Add the onion and sauté for 2 to 3 minutes, stirring frequently. Add the garlic and cook for another minute, still stirring. Stir in the bell pepper, carrot, and squash and cook for another 4 to 5 minutes, or until they start to soften.

4. Add the reserved sauce, scallions, and the drained noodles. Reduce the heat to low and cook for 2 to 3 minutes to warm through. Serve topped with basil and with lime wedges, if desired.

VARIATION: Most Thai restaurants will give you multiple heat levels to choose from, ranging from mild to hot. And then there is "Thai hot," which some restaurants won't serve you until you've proven you can handle the regular hot! If you want more heat, you can swap out the sriracha for a hotter sauce (look for brands made with Thai bird chiles).

CHILI-GARLIC NOODLES

SERVES 4 / **PREP TIME:** 15 minutes / **COOK TIME:** 15 minutes
NUT-FREE

These noodles are so saucy and full of flavor, I make them at least once a month. They're also great for using up vegetables, so feel free to substitute what you have on hand. As for the noodles, any rice noodle will work, although I tend to favor thick pad thai style.

FOR THE SAUCE

¼ cup plus 2 tablespoons soy sauce

3 tablespoons hoisin sauce

2 tablespoons water

1 tablespoon sambal oelek

1 teaspoon sugar

FOR THE NOODLES

1 (14-ounce) package rice noodles

1 to 2 tablespoons vegetable oil

1 medium zucchini, cut into thin 2-inch-long strips

1 large carrot, julienned

1 bell pepper, any color, cut into thin 2-inch-long strips

½ sweet onion, cut into thin 2-inch-long strips

1 teaspoon minced garlic

2 or 3 scallions, sliced, for topping (optional)

Crushed salted peanuts, for topping (optional)

Lime wedges, for serving (optional)

1. In a small bowl, make the sauce by whisking together the soy sauce, hoisin sauce, water, sambal oelek, and sugar. Set aside.

2. Cook the noodles according to the package directions. Drain and rinse in cold water.

3. Meanwhile, in a medium saucepan, heat the oil over medium-high heat. Add the zucchini, carrot, bell pepper, and onion and sauté for 5 to 6 minutes, stirring frequently. Add the garlic and continue to cook for another 2 to 3 minutes.

4. Reduce the heat to medium-low and stir in the noodles and sauce. Simmer, covered, for 2 to 3 minutes to heat through. Stir. If the sauce is too thick, add 1 to 2 tablespoons of water. If desired, top with the scallions and peanuts and serve with lime wedges.

VARIATION: Sambal oelek is a spicy Indonesian paste made with chile peppers, garlic, onion, and other yummy stuff—and it's where this dish gets its amazing flavor! If you want to make this dish hotter, try increasing the amount to 2 tablespoons. Be sure to check ingredients, as not all brands are vegan, and because it is garlicky you may want to reduce the amount of garlic you add in step 3.

TRIPLE-SQUASH MANICOTTI

SERVES 6 / PREP TIME: 20 minutes / **COOK TIME:** 40 minutes
NUT-FREE OPTION / SOY-FREE OPTION

Baked pasta dishes that come out of the oven smothered in bubbling cheese and sauce are the best. This manicotti dish is perfect for Sunday night family dinner, served with a big ol' salad, some crispy garlic bread, and plenty of love.

12 manicotti shells

1 medium zucchini, chopped

1 medium summer squash, chopped

2 teaspoons olive oil

½ teaspoon salt, plus more for sprinkling

¼ teaspoon black pepper, plus more for sprinkling

3 cups butternut squash puree, divided

2 cups vegan ricotta cheese

1 (24-ounce) jar pasta sauce, divided

1 cup shredded vegan mozzarella cheese

Fresh basil (optional)

1. Preheat the oven to 400°F.

2. Cook the manicotti to al dente according to the package directions. Drain and lay out in a single layer and set aside until you're ready to stuff them.

3. In a medium bowl, toss together the zucchini, summer squash, olive oil, salt, and pepper. In a small bowl, stir together 1 cup of the butternut squash puree and the ricotta.

4. Spread ¼ cup of the pasta sauce across the bottom of a 9-by-13-inch baking dish. Using a spoon or a zip-top plastic bag with a corner snipped off, fill the manicotti with the ricotta-butternut mixture. Arrange the manicotti in a single layer in the baking dish. Spread the remaining 2 cups of butternut puree on top with the back of a spoon or a silicone spatula. Sprinkle the diced squash and zucchini mixture evenly across the top, then cover with the remaining pasta sauce. Top with the mozzarella and sprinkle with salt and pepper to taste.

5. Cover the dish with aluminum foil and bake for 30 minutes, or until the cheese is melted and the sauce is bubbling. Let sit for 5 minutes before serving. Top with fresh basil, if desired.

MAKE AHEAD: The manicotti can be stuffed and assembled the day before to save time. Cover the dish tightly with foil and refrigerate until you're ready to bake.

DIY: Make your own ricotta (page 141).

PASTA PRIMAVERA

SERVES 6 / PREP TIME: 20 minutes / **COOK TIME:** 15 minutes
NUT-FREE OPTION / SOY-FREE OPTION

For a pasta dish with so many vegetables, primavera still seems decadent—must be the butter! You can use your favorite pasta or whatever you have on hand, but a short pasta works best to catch all the yummy sauce.

1 (16-ounce) box penne pasta

4 tablespoons vegan butter

1 teaspoon minced garlic

½ teaspoon onion powder

2 carrots, cut into thin 2-inch-long matchsticks

1 zucchini, diced

1 bell pepper, any color, diced

2 cups broccoli florets

⅔ cup frozen peas

12 cherry tomatoes, halved

2 teaspoons lemon juice

½ cup nutritional yeast, plus more for serving

1 to 2 tablespoons olive or avocado oil (optional)

¼ teaspoon salt

¼ teaspoon black pepper

10 to 12 fresh basil leaves, torn (optional)

⅛ to ¼ teaspoon red pepper flakes (optional)

1. Cook the pasta to al dente according to the package directions. Reserving ¼ cup of the cooking water, drain the pasta, and set aside.

2. Meanwhile, in a large saucepan, melt the butter over medium-high heat. Add the minced garlic and onion powder and sauté for 1 to 2 minutes, stirring frequently.

3. Stir the carrot, zucchini, bell pepper, broccoli, and peas into the saucepan, along with 1 to 2 tablespoons of the pasta cooking water. Reduce the heat to low, cover, and cook the veggies for 6 to 8 minutes, stirring occasionally. Add more pasta water if the pan starts to dry out.

〉〉

4. When the veggies are tender, stir in the drained pasta, tomatoes, lemon juice, and nutritional yeast. Let sit over low heat for another 2 to 3 minutes to warm through. Depending on how much liquid your veggies release while cooking, you may or may not want to add the olive oil or additional pasta water. Stir in the salt and black pepper. Serve topped with the basil leaves and red pepper flakes, as well as extra nutritional yeast, if desired.

VARIATION: There are no rules about what kind of veggies you use here. Sugar snap peas, cauliflower, and even cubed butternut squash are all great choices, so go with what you love.

DIY: Make your own butter (page 146).

CHAPTER EIGHT

DEEP-DISH BAKES

· · · · · ·

VEGETABLE ALFREDO BAKE

SERVES 6 / **PREP TIME:** 5 minutes / **COOK TIME:** 55 minutes
NUT-FREE OPTION / SOY-FREE OPTION

This filling pasta dish couldn't be much easier to make, and I love that the pasta cooks in the oven. It's the ultimate dump 'n' bake masterpiece, and no one will suspect that you didn't spend the whole afternoon in the kitchen.

1 (16-ounce) box bow-tie pasta

3 cups vegan Alfredo sauce

3 cups vegetable broth

1½ cups broccoli florets

½ cup frozen peas

1 cup shredded vegan mozzarella cheese

½ teaspoon salt, plus more to taste

¼ teaspoon black pepper

Fresh basil, for topping (optional)

1. Preheat the oven to 425°F.

2. In a 9-by-13-inch baking dish, stir together the dry pasta, Alfredo sauce, broth, broccoli, and peas. Cover with aluminum foil and bake for 30 to 40 minutes, until the pasta is al dente.

3. Remove the foil and cover the top of the pasta with the mozzarella, salt, and pepper. The pasta may look watery at this point, but it will thicken as it continues to bake.

4. Return the dish to the oven and bake for another 10 to 15 minutes, until the cheese has melted and the sauce is the desired consistency. Serve topped with fresh basil, if desired.

VARIATION: Add your favorite veggies or whatever you have on hand. Spinach, diced carrots, or diced sweet potatoes are all delicious.

DIY: Make your own Alfredo sauce (page 142; use the cashew-based version).

BAKED MAC 'N' CHEESE

SERVES 6 / PREP TIME: 10 minutes / **COOK TIME:** 40 minutes
NUT-FREE OPTION / SOY-FREE OPTION

There is something so comforting about this Baked Mac 'n' Cheese, which I believe is best enjoyed with good friends. I like to sprinkle a little extra cheese and chili powder on top for some zing!

Nonstick cooking spray

1 (16-ounce) box pasta shells

3 tablespoons vegan butter

3 tablespoons all-purpose flour

2½ cups unsweetened nondairy milk

½ teaspoon onion powder

½ teaspoon garlic powder

½ teaspoon salt

¼ teaspoon black pepper

¼ teaspoon chili powder, plus more for topping (optional)

2 cups shredded vegan cheddar cheese

1 cup panko bread crumbs

1. Preheat the oven to 350°F. Lightly mist a 7-by-11-inch baking dish with cooking spray.

2. Cook the pasta for a couple of minutes less than the time on the package directions. Drain and set aside.

3. In a medium saucepan, melt the butter over medium-high heat. Stir in the flour and cook for 2 to 3 minutes, stirring frequently. Slowly pour in the milk, stirring the whole time. Add the onion powder, garlic powder, salt, pepper, and chili powder (if using). Let the mixture bubble for 2 to 3 minutes, until thick. Add the cheese, and when it has fully melted, add the drained pasta, stirring until combined.

4. Pour the mixture into the prepared baking dish, cover with the panko, and sprinkle on more chili powder, if desired. Bake for 20 to 25 minutes, until the sides bubble. Serve immediately.

DIY: Make your own butter (page 146) and milk (page 140).

CHEDDAR-BROCCOLI RICE CASSEROLE

SERVES 4 / **PREP TIME:** 10 minutes / **COOK TIME:** 30 minutes
NUT-FREE OPTION / **SOY-FREE OPTION**

This casserole makes a great meal or side dish, and it would be perfect as part of a holiday spread. The buttery cracker topping and all the melted cheese makes it extra decadent and special.

2 tablespoons olive oil
½ sweet onion, diced
½ teaspoon minced garlic
2½ cups vegetable broth
1 cup long-grain white rice
2½ cups broccoli florets
1½ cups shredded vegan cheddar cheese

1½ cups sliced vegan chick'n (unbreaded) or Mouthwatering Seitan "Meat" (page 147)
1 cup crumbled vegan butter crackers, such as Ritz
2 tablespoons vegan butter, melted

1. Preheat the oven to 400°F.

2. In a Dutch oven or other ovenproof pan, heat the oil over medium-high heat. Add the onion and sauté for 2 to 3 minutes, stirring frequently. Add the garlic and cook for 1 more minute.

3. Increase the heat to high and stir in the broth and rice. Cover and bring to a boil. Reduce the heat to low and simmer for 12 minutes.

4. Stir in the broccoli, cover, and simmer for 6 to 8 more minutes, until the broccoli is barely tender and the rice is cooked. Stir ½ cup of cheese and the chick'n into the rice mixture. Sprinkle the remaining 1 cup of cheese across the top. Transfer to the oven and bake for 10 minutes, or until the cheese is melted. Meanwhile, combine the crackers and melted butter.

5. Take the pan out of the oven and turn the oven to low broil. Spoon the crumbs over the top, return to the oven, and broil for 30 to 60 seconds—keeping a close eye so it doesn't burn—until the topping is a light golden brown. Let cool for a few minutes before serving.

LIGHTEN UP: Instead of the crackers and butter, try topping with ½ cup panko bread crumbs and spritzing lightly with cooking spray.

DIY: Make your own butter (page 146).

UN-STUFFED PEPPER CASSEROLE

SERVES 6 / **PREP TIME:** 10 minutes / **COOK TIME:** 35 minutes
GLUTEN-FREE / NUT-FREE OPTION / SOY-FREE OPTION

This casserole gives you all the flavor of stuffed peppers with much less work. Using yellow or red bell peppers will make the dish a little sweeter and adding a jalapeño pepper (especially if you don't remove all the ribs!) will give it a nice, spicy edginess.

1 tablespoon olive oil

1 small sweet onion, chopped

½ teaspoon minced garlic

2 bell peppers, any color, chopped

1 jalapeño pepper, seeded and chopped (optional)

1 (15-ounce) can black beans, drained and rinsed

½ teaspoon smoked paprika

½ teaspoon ground cumin

½ teaspoon salt

¼ teaspoon black pepper

1 (14.5-ounce) can diced tomatoes, undrained

1 cup vegetable broth

½ cup long-grain white rice

1 cup shredded vegan cheddar cheese

Fresh parsley, for garnish (optional)

Vegan sour cream, for serving (optional)

1. Preheat the oven to 400°F.

2. In a Dutch oven or other ovenproof pan, heat the oil over medium-high heat. Add the onion and sauté for 2 to 3 minutes, stirring frequently. Add the garlic and cook for 1 more minute.

3. Add the bell peppers, jalapeño (if using), beans, smoked paprika, cumin, salt, and black pepper and cook for 4 to 5 minutes, until the peppers begin to soften, stirring occasionally.

4. Stir in the tomatoes and their juices, broth, and rice. Cover and cook for another 12 to 15 minutes, until the rice has absorbed the liquid. If necessary, add 2 to 3 tablespoons of water and cook the rice for a few minutes longer.

》》

5. Cover the top of the mixture with the cheese and transfer to the oven. Bake for 10 minutes, or until the cheese has melted. Serve topped with fresh parsley and sour cream, if desired.

VARIATION: To make these "Buffalo" stuffed peppers, skip the paprika and cumin. Add the diced tomatoes, but drain them first, and add ¼ to ½ cup Buffalo sauce after the rice is cooked, at the end of step 4. Top with pepper jack cheese instead of cheddar.

DIY: Make your own sour cream (page 136).

VEGGIE LOVER'S PIZZA CASSEROLE

SERVES 8 / PREP TIME: 15 minutes / **COOK TIME:** 25 minutes
NUT-FREE OPTION / SOY-FREE OPTION

Here's a fun take on pizza that uses pasta instead of dough and bakes it all in a casserole! This dish is simple to make gluten-free, just by using the right pasta. Feel free to substitute your favorite veggie toppings.

Nonstick cooking spray
½ (16-ounce) box elbow macaroni pasta
2 small bell peppers, different
  colors, chopped
1 sweet onion, chopped
½ cup sliced button or baby bella
  mushrooms
1 (14-ounce) can artichoke hearts, drained
1 (2.25-ounce) can sliced black
  olives, drained

1 (24-ounce) jar marinara sauce
1 teaspoon dried oregano, plus more
  for topping
½ teaspoon garlic powder
½ teaspoon salt
½ teaspoon black pepper
1½ cups shredded vegan
  mozzarella cheese
Fresh basil, for topping (optional)
Red pepper flakes, for topping (optional)

1. Preheat the oven to 350°F. Lightly mist a 9-by-13-inch baking dish with cooking spray.

2. Cook the pasta to al dente according to the package directions.

3. Drain the pasta and return it to the pot. Stir in the bell peppers, onion, mushrooms, artichoke hearts, olives, marinara, oregano, garlic powder, salt, and black pepper. Pour the mixture into the prepared baking dish and top with the cheese and an extra sprinkle of oregano.

4. Bake for 20 to 25 minutes, until the cheese is melted and the veggies have softened. Serve topped with fresh basil and red pepper flakes, if desired.

VARIATION: Turn this into a (Mock) Meat Lover's Pizza Casserole by substituting your favorite vegan pepperoni and sausage for half of the veggies.

TERIYAKI TOFU AND RICE CASSEROLE

SERVES 6 / PREP TIME: 15 minutes / **COOK TIME:** 50 minutes
NUT-FREE

This casserole is the vegan answer to those meat-heavy teriyaki dishes at your local take-out place. You can save time and effort with those handy packages of microwavable rice and frozen "stir-fry" vegetable mixes without sacrificing any flavor.

FOR THE TOFU

Nonstick cooking spray

1 tablespoon soy sauce

1 tablespoon vegetable oil

1 tablespoon cornstarch

¼ teaspoon ground ginger

1 (14-ounce) package extra-firm tofu, well pressed and cut into small cubes

FOR THE CASSEROLE

2 cups water

1 cup long-grain white rice, rinsed

4 cups frozen chopped stir-fry vegetables (water chestnuts, carrots, snow peas, broccoli, etc.)

2 cups teriyaki sauce

½ cup canned diced pineapple

3 scallions, thinly sliced

1. Preheat the oven to 400°F. Lightly mist a 7-by-11-inch baking dish with cooking spray.

2. In a bowl, whisk together the soy sauce, vegetable oil, cornstarch, and ginger. Toss in the tofu to coat.

3. Transfer the tofu to the baking dish, spread in a single layer, and bake for 30 to 35 minutes, flipping once halfway through. The tofu should be lightly browned and crispy. (Leave the oven on.)

4. Meanwhile, bring the water to a boil in a small saucepan. Stir in the rice, cover, and bring back to a simmer. Reduce the heat and simmer, covered, for 18 minutes. Check to see if the rice is done; let simmer for 1 to 2 more minutes, if necessary. Drain off any excess water.

5. When the tofu is done, add the rice, stir-fry vegetables, teriyaki sauce, and pineapple to the baking dish and stir to combine. Return to the oven and bake for 15 minutes, or until heated through. Serve topped with the scallions.

MAKE AHEAD: If you want to do the bulk of the work ahead of time, bake the tofu, cook the rice, and combine all the ingredients in the baking dish. Cover tightly with aluminum foil and refrigerate until ready to bake and serve. The dish will need 20 to 25 minutes in the oven to heat through after being refrigerated.

COCONUT CURRY SWEET POTATO CASSEROLE

SERVES 8 / **PREP TIME:** 15 minutes / **COOK TIME:** 50 minutes
GLUTEN-FREE / **NUT-FREE** / **SOY-FREE**

I love the combination of coconut milk and curry spices so much that I've attempted to put it in nearly everything. My favorite vegetable by far to pair with this sauce is sweet potato; it's hearty, filling, and so healthy. I also love this casserole because the rice bakes in the oven, making it extra easy.

FOR THE CASSEROLE

Nonstick cooking spray

2 sweet potatoes, peeled and chopped

1 bell pepper, any color, chopped

3 cups cauliflower florets

1½ cups long-grain white rice

FOR THE CURRY SAUCE

1 (14-ounce) can coconut milk, well shaken

1½ cups vegetable broth

2 tablespoons curry powder

2 tablespoons lime juice

2 teaspoons light brown sugar

1 teaspoon ground ginger

1 teaspoon minced garlic

1 teaspoon ground coriander

½ teaspoon salt

1. Preheat the oven to 375°F. Lightly coat a 9-by-13-inch baking dish with cooking spray.

2. In the prepared baking dish, stir together the sweet potatoes, bell pepper, cauliflower, and rice.

3. In a small bowl, make the sauce by whisking together the coconut milk, broth, curry powder, lime juice, sugar, ginger, garlic, coriander, and salt.

4. Pour the curry sauce over the vegetables, cover the dish with aluminum foil, and carefully transfer it to the oven. Bake for 45 to 50 minutes, until the rice is tender and much of the liquid has been absorbed. For less liquid, let it cook for 4 to 5 more minutes without the foil. Let cool for a few minutes before serving.

LIGHTEN UP: If you're looking to reduce the fat content, you can use light coconut milk. It is a little less flavorful but works just as well.

CHEESEBURGER CASSEROLE

SERVES 4 / **PREP TIME:** 20 minutes / **COOK TIME:** 30 minutes
NUT-FREE OPTION / SOY-FREE OPTION

I have turned (vegan) cheeseburgers into quesadillas and even pizza. So why not a casserole? This dish is easy to make, and the leftovers are even better after a day or two in the fridge.

Nonstick cooking spray

1 tablespoon vegetable oil

½ sweet onion, chopped

2 cups vegan "beef" crumbles or
   2 loaves Mouthwatering Seitan "Meat"
   (page 147), crumbled

1 tablespoon vegan
   Worcestershire sauce

1 teaspoon Italian seasoning

½ teaspoon salt

¼ teaspoon black pepper

¼ teaspoon chili powder

1¼ cups canned diced tomatoes,
   undrained

1 cup vegetable broth

1 cup pasta shells or elbows

¾ cup vegan sour cream

1½ cups shredded vegan
   cheddar cheese

½ cup dill pickle chips, roughly chopped
   (optional)

1. Preheat the oven to 400°F. Lightly coat a 7-by-11-inch baking dish with cooking spray.

2. In a large saucepan, heat the oil over medium-high heat. Add the onion, "beef" crumbles, Worcestershire, Italian seasoning, salt, pepper, and chili powder. Cook for 6 to 8 minutes, stirring frequently, until the onion is soft and the crumbles have browned.

3. Stir in the tomatoes with their juices, broth, and pasta. Bring to a boil, then reduce the heat to low. Cover and simmer, stirring once or twice, for 8 to 10 minutes, until the pasta is al dente. Remove from the heat and stir in the sour cream.

4. Pour about half of the "hamburger" mixture into the prepared baking dish, then sprinkle half of the cheese on top. Add the remaining "hamburger" mixture, and then the rest of the cheese.

5. Bake for 10 to 12 minutes, until the cheese is melted and the casserole is bubbling. Let cool slightly before serving topped with the pickle chips, if desired.

VARIATION: Chop up half a batch of Super Smoky Seitan Bacon (page 149) and add it to the top with the pickles to make this a Bacon Cheeseburger Casserole!

DIY: Make your own sour cream (page 136).

CRISPY POTATO HOTDISH

SERVES 6 / PREP TIME: 20 minutes, plus 4 hours to soak / **COOK TIME:** 45 minutes
GLUTEN-FREE OPTION / SOY-FREE OPTION

My friend Denise is from Minnesota and tells stories about the hotdish of her childhood, covered in tater tots or crushed potato chips. Having grown up in New England the idea sounded crazy to me ... until I tried it. Now I can't get enough! Veggies and vegan meat smothered in a creamy cashew sauce, topped with tater tots and cheese—does it get any better?

FOR THE SAUCE

- 2 cups vegetable broth
- ¾ cup raw cashews, soaked in water for at least 4 hours, drained, and rinsed
- 2 tablespoons cornstarch
- 1 teaspoon mustard powder
- 1 teaspoon dried parsley
- ½ teaspoon salt
- ¼ teaspoon black pepper

FOR THE HOTDISH

- 2 tablespoons vegetable oil
- ½ sweet onion, diced
- 1 teaspoon minced garlic
- 2 cups vegan "beef" crumbles or 2 loaves Mouthwatering Seitan "Meat" (page 147), crumbled
- 2 carrots, diced
- 1½ cups broccoli florets
- 2 to 3 cups frozen tater tots
- 1 cup shredded vegan cheddar cheese
- Chopped fresh parsley, for garnish (optional)

1. Preheat the oven to 400°F.

2. In a blender or food processor, make the sauce by combining the broth, cashews, cornstarch, mustard powder, parsley, salt, and pepper. Blend until smooth.

3. In a Dutch oven or other ovenproof pan, heat the oil over medium-high heat. Add the onion and sauté for 2 to 3 minutes, stirring frequently. Add the garlic and cook for 1 more minute. Stir in the "beef" crumbles and sauté for another 4 to 5 minutes, until they start to brown.

4. Remove the pan from the heat and stir in the carrots and broccoli. Pour the cashew sauce over the top, then add a layer of tater tots (the amount needed will depend on the size of your pan). Sprinkle the cheese over the top.

5. Transfer the pan to the oven and bake for 30 to 35 minutes, until the tater tots are a nice golden brown and the inside of the hotdish is bubbling. Serve topped with fresh parsley, if desired, and sprinkled with salt and pepper to taste.

LIGHTEN UP: You can skip the cheese to save on calories or substitute pinto beans for the mock meat.

CHEESY VEGGIE CASSEROLE

SERVES 6 / PREP TIME: 20 minutes / **COOK TIME:** 50 minutes
NUT-FREE OPTION / SOY-FREE OPTION

This casserole is basically mac 'n' cheese's virtuous cousin. You still get that gooey, melty cheese sauce . . . but with four kinds of veggies. Serve with a side of garlic bread to really nail that comfort-food vibe!

Nonstick cooking spray

1 large sweet potato, peeled and chopped

6 cups broccoli and cauliflower florets

2 tablespoons vegan butter

3 tablespoons all-purpose flour

2 cups unsweetened nondairy milk

1 (10-ounce) package frozen butternut squash puree, thawed

2 cups shredded vegan cheddar cheese

1 teaspoon salt

1 teaspoon chili powder

1½ cups plain dried bread crumbs

1. Preheat the oven to 350°F. Lightly mist a 9-by-13-inch baking dish with cooking spray.

2. In a large pot of boiling water, cook the sweet potato for 6 to 8 minutes, until just soft. Add the broccoli and cauliflower, remove from the heat, and let the veggies sit in the hot water for 1 to 2 minutes. Drain, reserving 1 cup of the cooking liquid.

3. Return the pot to medium heat and melt the butter. Whisk in the flour to create a roux, stirring constantly for about 1 minute until thickened. Whisk in the milk and reserved cooking liquid. Continue to stir frequently for 5 to 7 minutes, until thickened.

4. Reduce the heat to low and stir in the squash puree, cheese, salt, and chili powder. Stir until the cheese is melted, then fold in the vegetables.

5. Pour the veggie mixture into the prepared baking dish, spreading it out evenly. Top with the bread crumbs, spritz the top lightly with cooking spray, and bake for 30 minutes, or until the cheese is bubbling and the vegetables are tender. Put the casserole under the broiler on low for 30 to 60 seconds before serving for a crispier top.

VARIATION: Carrots, red potatoes, and parsnips make great veggie swaps if you want to change it up a little. If you use frozen veggies instead of fresh, you can skip adding them to the boiling water in step 1. Instead, simply allow them to thaw before folding them into the cheese sauce in step 4.

DIY: Make your own butter (page 146) and milk (page 140).

PEANUT BUTTER–BANANA MILKSHAKE · 125

CHAPTER NINE

SOMETHING SWEET

. . . . . .

CHOCOLATE CHIP COOKIE DOUGH DIP

SERVES 8 / PREP TIME: 5 minutes

NUT-FREE OPTION / SOY-FREE OPTION

This sweet treat comes together in just 5 minutes, making it one of the easiest desserts ever. It's perfect for those hot summer nights when you want something sweet, but don't want to turn on the oven.

½ cup vegan butter, at room temperature

½ cup powdered sugar

¼ cup packed light brown sugar

8 ounces vegan cream cheese

1½ teaspoons vanilla extract

½ teaspoon salt

1½ cups vegan chocolate chips

Graham crackers or pretzels, for dipping

1. Using a hand mixer, cream together the butter, powdered sugar, and brown sugar. Beat in the cream cheese and vanilla until combined.

2. Fold in the salt and chocolate chips, then serve with graham crackers or pretzels.

MAKE AHEAD: Make this dessert up to 2 days ahead of time and keep refrigerated in an airtight container. Stir well before serving.

DIY: Make your own butter (page 146) and cream cheese (page 138).

PEANUT BUTTER-BANANA MILKSHAKE

SERVES 1 / PREP TIME: 5 minutes
GLUTEN-FREE / SOY-FREE OPTION

Ice cream without any of the guilt: That is the magic of bananas! During the summer, I inhale banana "nice cream" nearly every day, sometimes with a splash of vanilla and sometimes with more complicated toppings. But every now and then what I really crave is a milkshake... with peanut butter and chocolate, of course! The trick is to choose bananas that are super ripe, as they are the sweetest. If yours are ripe enough, you won't need the maple syrup sweetener.

2 bananas, sliced and frozen

¾ cup sweetened or unsweetened nondairy milk

¼ cup creamy peanut butter

1 teaspoon real maple syrup (optional)

Coconut whipped cream, for topping (optional)

Chocolate syrup, for topping (optional)

1. In a blender or food processor, pulse the frozen banana pieces for 1 to 2 minutes, until creamy.

2. Add the milk, peanut butter, and maple syrup (if using). Continue to blend for another 30 seconds, or until completely smooth. Add an extra teaspoon of milk if needed to reach your desired consistency.

3. Transfer the milkshake to a large glass. If desired, top with coconut whip and chocolate syrup.

   VARIATION: Frozen strawberries, raspberries, or other fruit you have in the freezer make tasty additions, too!

   DIY: Make your own milk (page 140) and coconut whipped cream (page 137).

BUTTERSCOTCH PUDDING

SERVES 4 / **PREP TIME:** 5 minutes, plus 1 hour to chill / **COOK TIME:** 10 minutes

GLUTEN-FREE / NUT-FREE OPTION / SOY-FREE OPTION

The taste of butterscotch reminds me of my great-grandmother. She always had those mouthwatering hard candies on the table in her living room, and I would stare at them until she offered me one. This pudding version is delicious on its own or topped with vegan whipped cream!

2 tablespoons vegan butter

½ cup packed light brown sugar

½ teaspoon salt, plus more
  to taste

¼ cup cornstarch

3 cups unsweetened cashew or
  coconut milk

1 teaspoon vanilla extract

Coconut whipped cream, for topping
  (optional)

1. In a saucepan, melt the butter over medium heat. Stir in the brown sugar with a silicone spatula. Reduce the heat to medium-low and simmer for 1 to 2 minutes, stirring almost constantly.

2. Reduce the heat to low. Stir in the salt and cornstarch, then switch to a whisk. Whisk constantly while slowly adding the milk.

3. Switch back to the silicone spatula and increase the heat to medium-low. Stirring frequently, let the pudding come to a simmer and cook for about 1 minute, or until thick. Remove from the heat and stir in the vanilla.

4. Pour the pudding into a serving bowl and cover with plastic wrap, pressing it gently against the surface of the pudding to prevent a skin from forming. Refrigerate the pudding for at least 1 hour before serving, or until it is completely set. Serve as-is or with the coconut whip, if desired.

MAKE AHEAD: This pudding will stay fresh and yummy in an airtight container, refrigerated, for up to 3 days.

DIY: Make your own butter (page 146) and coconut whipped cream (page 137).

CHOCOLATE MOUSSE

Avocados are such a trend that they've become a staple in everyone's diet. So of course, avocados have made their way into dessert. Creamy and luscious, they make a perfect base for this decadent Chocolate Mousse— so much so that you won't even taste the avocado!

½ cup vegan dark or milk chocolate chips

1 teaspoon coconut oil

1 small avocado, halved, peeled, and pitted

1 cup silken tofu

3 tablespoons powdered sugar

½ teaspoon vanilla extract

⅛ teaspoon salt

Shredded coconut, for topping (optional)

Coconut whipped cream, for topping (optional)

1. Set a heatproof glass bowl over a small saucepan of simmering water. Add the chocolate chips and coconut oil and stir until completely melted and combined.

2. Scoop the avocado into a blender or processor. Add the melted chocolate, tofu, sugar, vanilla, and salt and blend until completely smooth.

3. Transfer the mousse to a serving bowl and refrigerate for 30 minutes, or until ready to serve. If desired, top with shredded coconut and coconut whip.

VARIATION: Enjoy this mousse as part of a parfait by layering it with sliced banana and strawberries, graham cracker crumbs, and vegan whipped cream.

DIY: Make your own coconut whipped cream (page 137).

CHOCOLATE-BANANA BREAD PUDDING

SERVES 8 / **PREP TIME:** 15 minutes / **COOK TIME:** 40 minutes
NUT-FREE OPTION / **SOY-FREE OPTION**

The real story behind my love of bread pudding has to do with my Nana. One day she took me to lunch at one of those buffet restaurants, and after we were seated, I realized she had brought Tupperware in her purse to steal bread pudding and bring it home with her! It was my job to bring plates and plates of it to the table. I ended up bringing more than could fit in the Tupperware, and so I had to eat the rest. Thankfully, I discovered that I liked it! I highly recommend serving it hot with creamy vegan ice cream.

Nonstick cooking spray

2 bananas

1¾ cups unsweetened nondairy milk

½ cup packed light brown sugar

1 teaspoon vanilla extract

½ teaspoon ground cinnamon

½ cup vegan chocolate chips

10 slices stale white bread, cut into 1-inch cubes

Chocolate or vanilla vegan ice cream, for serving (optional)

1. Preheat the oven to 350°F. Lightly mist a 7-by-11-inch baking dish with cooking spray.

2. In a large bowl, mash the bananas with the back of a fork, then whisk in the milk to combine. Whisk in the brown sugar, vanilla, and cinnamon. Add the chocolate chips, then toss the bread cubes in the mixture to coat.

3. Spoon the bread pudding into the prepared baking dish. Bake for 35 to 40 minutes, or until the top is a light golden brown and the pudding is cooked through. If the top is getting dark but the pudding isn't done yet, cover it loosely with aluminum foil. Serve topped with ice cream, if desired.

VARIATION: For PB&J bread pudding, whisk ½ cup creamy peanut butter in with the milk in step 2 and omit the chocolate chips. Serve topped with a schmear of your favorite jam.

DIY: Make your own milk (page 140).

CHERRY TURNOVERS

MAKES 8 TURNOVERS / **PREP TIME:** 20 minutes / **COOK TIME:** 18 minutes
NUT-FREE OPTION / **SOY-FREE OPTION**

These turnovers are way easier than baking a pie but just as delicious. Plus, you can easily substitute whatever type of filling you're craving. In the fall, I love to use apple!

1 (17.3-ounce) box frozen puff pastry, thawed per the package directions
1 (21-ounce) can cherry pie filling
1½ cups powdered sugar

2 tablespoons unsweetened nondairy milk
1 teaspoon vanilla extract

1. Preheat the oven to 400°F. Line a rimmed baking sheet with parchment paper.

2. Cut each sheet of puff pastry into quarters. You want each piece to be roughly 5 inches square, so either trim to about that size or, if needed, use a rolling pin to roll out to the correct size.

3. Spoon 2 tablespoons of the filling onto the center of each square. Use your finger to run water around the edge of the pastry, then fold it into a triangle. Crimp the edges firmly with a fork, and score the top of each to allow steam to vent.

4. Place the turnovers on the prepared baking sheet and bake for 15 to 18 minutes, or until the pastry is a very light golden brown. Remove the turnovers from the oven and let cool completely.

5. While the turnovers are cooling, whisk together the sugar, milk, and vanilla. Drizzle the glaze over the tops of the turnovers and serve.

LIGHTEN UP: If you're looking to go a little lighter with the sugar, skip the glaze. The filling is sweet enough on its own!

DIY: Make your own milk (page 140).

CRISPY PEANUT BUTTER AND BOURBON BUCKEYES

MAKES 35 BUCKEYES / PREP TIME: 30 minutes, plus 30 minutes to chill
GLUTEN-FREE / SOY-FREE OPTION

A popular treat, especially in the Midwest, buckeyes are so named because they resemble the seed of the Ohio buckeye tree. You can skip the bourbon, but please don't skip the millet—it adds a wonderfully toasty little crunch. These do take a bit of work, so I suggest doubling the recipe and freezing the extras for later!

3½ teaspoons coconut oil, divided

⅓ cup millet, rinsed and dried

¾ cup creamy peanut butter

½ cup vegan butter, at room temperature

½ teaspoon vanilla extract

2 tablespoons bourbon (optional)

2½ cups powdered sugar

1 cup vegan dark chocolate chips

1. Line a rimmed baking sheet with wax paper and set aside.

2. In a small pan, melt 1 teaspoon of coconut oil over medium heat. Add the millet and stir until it turns golden and smells toasty, 4 to 5 minutes. Set aside to cool.

3. In a large bowl, combine the peanut butter, butter, and vanilla. Using a hand mixer, beat the mixture on low until completely combined. Add the bourbon (if using), then slowly add the powdered sugar, continuing to mix on low until combined. Fold in the millet.

4. Scoop the peanut butter mixture into 1- to 1½-inch balls and place them on the prepared baking sheet. Place the baking sheet in the freezer and let the peanut butter balls chill for at least 30 minutes, or until they feel solid to the touch.

5. When the peanut butter balls are ready, set a heatproof glass bowl over a small saucepan of simmering water. Add the chocolate chips and remaining 2½ teaspoons of coconut oil to the bowl and stir until completely melted and combined. Remove from the heat. Using a toothpick, dip each ball into the chocolate, then return to the baking sheet. Keep refrigerated or frozen until the chocolate has hardened and you are ready to serve.

MAKE AHEAD: Steps 1 to 4 can be done up to a few days in advance. Just make sure the balls are tightly covered in the freezer until you're ready to coat them in the chocolate.

DIY: Make your own butter (page 146).

CHAPTER TEN

DIY STAPLES

COOL 'N' CREAMY VEGAN SOUR CREAM

MAKES 1¼ CUPS / PREP TIME: 5 minutes, plus overnight to soak
GLUTEN-FREE / SOY-FREE OPTION

I put sour cream on a lot of things. Spicy dishes such as Buffalo Chick'n Taquitos (page 76) and Taco Bites (page 73) are made even better with the topping, but it's also good for adding to savory breakfast dishes, like a freshly made Veggieful Tofu Scramble (page 23)!

1 cup raw cashews, soaked in water overnight, drained, and rinsed
Juice of 1 lemon

¼ cup unsweetened nondairy milk, plus more as needed
1½ teaspoons apple cider vinegar
½ teaspoon salt, plus more as needed

In a blender, combine the cashews, lemon juice, milk, vinegar, and salt. Blend until completely smooth. Taste and add more salt to get the desired flavor. For thinner sour cream, add a little more milk.

MAKE AHEAD: This sour cream stays fresh for up to 6 days when refrigerated in an airtight container.

DIY: Make your own milk (page 140).

SWEET TOOTH COCONUT WHIPPED CREAM

MAKES 1½ CUPS / PREP TIME: 5 minutes, plus overnight to chill
GLUTEN-FREE / NUT-FREE / SOY-FREE

Make any dessert 10 times fancier with this easy and delicious whipped topping! You can whip it up in just a few minutes, especially if you always keep a can of coconut milk in the fridge, like I do. Pro tip: Store-brand coconut milks work best because they tend to have more coconut cream solidified in the can.

1 (14-ounce) can full-fat coconut milk, refrigerated overnight

¼ cup powdered sugar
½ teaspoon pure vanilla extract

1. Carefully, without shaking or jostling it, open the can of coconut milk and scoop the solidified cream into a chilled metal bowl. Use a handheld electric mixer to whip it for 30 to 45 seconds, until it becomes creamy and smooth.

2. Add the sugar and vanilla and continue to whip for another 30 to 60 seconds, until smooth. Refrigerate until you're ready to use; it'll firm more as it chills.

VARIATION: Make chocolate whipped cream by adding ¼ cup cocoa powder along with the sugar and vanilla.

MAKE AHEAD: Keep the leftovers in an airtight container in the refrigerator for up to 1 week.

THE CREAMIEST VEGAN CREAM CHEESE

MAKES 2 CUPS / PREP TIME: 5 minutes, plus overnight to soak
GLUTEN-FREE / SOY-FREE OPTION

When I first went vegan, there was no such thing as plant-based cream cheese in stores, and as a newbie vegan (and home cook), the recipes I found online seemed over my head. It was a dark time, for sure. But no longer! There are now many brands on the market—and it's also super easy to make your own.

3 cups raw cashews, soaked in water
  overnight, drained, and rinsed
½ to ¾ cup unsweetened nondairy milk

¼ cup lemon juice
1 tablespoon apple cider vinegar
1 teaspoon salt

In a blender, combine the cashews, ½ cup of milk, the lemon juice, vinegar, and salt. Blend until very smooth. Add more milk, 1 tablespoon at a time, to get the desired consistency.

VARIATION: Add 1 to 2 tablespoons chopped fresh chives.

MAKE AHEAD: Refrigerate the cream cheese in an airtight container for up to 4 days.

DIY: Make your own milk (page 140).

"NO EGGS ABOUT IT" VEGAN MAYONNAISE

MAKES 2 CUPS / PREP TIME: 10 minutes
GLUTEN-FREE / NUT-FREE

I've always been one of those people who puts way too much mayo on everything, and I don't feel bad about it! There are lots of different DIY versions out there, but I like this one because the grapeseed oil makes it so rich and creamy, just like the "real" mayo I remember. Use the highest-quality oil you can afford; it will greatly enhance the flavor.

½ cup unsweetened soy milk

1½ cups grapeseed oil

1 tablespoon apple cider vinegar, plus more to taste

½ teaspoon mustard powder

½ teaspoon salt, plus more to taste

1. Pour the milk into a blender, cover, and turn the blender on to its lowest setting. Remove the steam vent cap from the lid and slowly pour the oil in. Continue to run the blender until you've reached your desired consistency.

2. Add the vinegar, mustard powder, and salt and pulse a few more times. Taste and add more salt or vinegar if desired. Cover and chill until ready to use.

   MAKE AHEAD: The mayo will stay fresh for up to 1 week when refrigerated in an airtight container.

SIMPLE OAT MILK

MAKES 4 CUPS / PREP TIME: 10 minutes

GLUTEN-FREE OPTION / NUT-FREE / SOY-FREE

These days, you can go to just about any grocery store and pick up high-quality, creamy nondairy milks at affordable prices. Even I tend to rely on these milks for my recipes since they're so easy and delicious. But to my DIYers out there or anyone who wants to know exactly what goes into their milk, this recipe for you. Even better, if you're like me and get halfway through making your morning coffee only to realize you're out of milk, you can whip up this recipe in a flash from ingredients already in your pantry! It's excellent cold, in a cup of tea, or in baking recipes.

4 cups water

1 cup rolled oats (do not soak beforehand)

¼ teaspoon salt

1 tablespoon real maple syrup (optional)

1. In a blender, combine the water, oats, salt, and maple syrup (if using) and blend for 30 to 60 seconds, just until well combined. Do not blend for more than a minute.

2. Pour the mixture through a nut milk bag, a fine-mesh sieve lined with cheesecloth, or a clean linen tea towel to strain.

   MAKE AHEAD: Keep refrigerated in an airtight container for up to 5 days. Shake before serving.

CRAVEABLE CASHEW RICOTTA

MAKES 1½ CUPS / PREP TIME: 10 minutes, plus 4 hours to soak

GLUTEN-FREE / SOY-FREE OPTION

This ricotta is easy to make and so versatile. Try it in Deconstructed Lasagna (page 89) or in Creamy Roasted Corn and Green Chile Dip (page 29). You can also mix it into any soup or pasta dish you want to make a little extra decadent.

1½ cups raw cashews, soaked for at least 4 hours, drained, and rinsed

½ cup unsweetened nondairy milk

2 tablespoons nutritional yeast

1 tablespoon apple cider vinegar

1 teaspoon garlic powder

1 teaspoon onion powder

¼ teaspoon salt

⅛ teaspoon black pepper

In a food processor, combine the cashews, milk, nutritional yeast, vinegar, garlic powder, onion powder, salt, and pepper and blend until thick and creamy. Taste and add more salt and pepper if desired.

MAKE AHEAD: Store in an airtight container in the refrigerator for up to 5 days.

DIY: Make your own milk (page 140).

THAT WAS VEGAN? ALFREDO SAUCE—TWO WAYS

MAKES 2 CUPS / PREP TIME: 10 minutes, plus 4 hours to soak (for the cashew sauce)
COOK TIME: 5 minutes
GLUTEN-FREE / NUT-FREE OPTION / SOY-FREE OPTION

Creamy? Check. Easy to make? Check. Perfect for your favorite pasta and veggie dishes? Absolutely! My favorite is the Fettuccine Alfredo with Roasted Vegetables (page 84), but this sauce is so versatile you can use it in all sorts of dishes. If you want to use this sauce in a baked recipe, like Vegetable Alfredo Bake (page 104), I recommend using the cashew preparation to stand up to the oven's heat and stay creamy and delicious.

TOFU ALFREDO

1 (14-ounce) package soft tofu, drained but not pressed
⅓ cup nutritional yeast
¼ cup unsweetened soy or cashew milk
½ teaspoon salt
¼ teaspoon garlic powder
¼ teaspoon Italian seasoning
½ cup shredded vegan mozzarella cheese (optional)

1. In a blender or food processor, combine the tofu, nutritional yeast, milk, salt, garlic powder, and Italian seasoning and blend until smooth.

2. Pour the sauce into a small saucepan and add the mozzarella cheese, if desired. Cook over medium-low heat, stirring frequently, for 4 to 5 minutes, until the cheese is melted and the sauce is warmed through.

CASHEW ALFREDO

2 cups raw cashews, soaked for at least 4 hours, drained, and rinsed

⅓ cup nutritional yeast

1½ to 2 cups unsweetened cashew or soy milk

1 tablespoon cornstarch

½ teaspoon salt

¼ teaspoon garlic powder

¼ teaspoon Italian seasoning

½ cup shredded vegan mozzarella cheese (optional)

1. In a blender or food processor, combine the cashews, nutritional yeast, milk, cornstarch, salt, garlic powder, and Italian seasoning and blend until smooth.

2. Pour the sauce into a small saucepan and add the mozzarella cheese, if desired. Cook over medium-low heat, stirring frequently, for 4 to 5 minutes, until the cheese is melted and the sauce is warmed through.

ZESTY VEGAN RANCH DRESSING

MAKES 1½ CUPS / PREP TIME: 10 minutes, plus overnight to soak
GLUTEN-FREE / SOY-FREE OPTION

Ranch is one of the most popular types of dressing, and for good reason—it's delicious! It provides a cool, creamy balance to spicy dishes such as Spicy Cauliflower Fritters (page 34). There are plenty of brands available in stores, but it's good to be able to make your own in a pinch.

½ cup unsweetened nondairy milk

2½ teaspoons apple cider
   vinegar, divided

¾ cup raw cashews, soaked overnight,
   drained, and rinsed

2 teaspoons dried parsley, or
   1½ tablespoons fresh parsley

1 teaspoon dried dill

1 teaspoon garlic powder

½ teaspoon onion powder

½ teaspoon agave nectar

½ teaspoon lemon juice

½ teaspoon salt

⅛ teaspoon black pepper

1. In a bowl, whisk together the milk and 1½ teaspoons of vinegar and let sit for a few minutes. The mixture should begin to curdle.

2. Pour into a blender or food processor, along with the cashews, parsley, dill, garlic powder, onion powder, agave nectar, lemon juice, salt, pepper, and the remaining 1 teaspoon of vinegar. Blend until completely smooth.

MAKE AHEAD: Store in an airtight container in the refrigerator for up to 5 days.

DIY: Make your own milk (page 140).

SO EASY VEGAN BUTTER

MAKES 2 CUPS / PREP TIME: 15 minutes, plus 1 hour to chill

GLUTEN-FREE / NUT-FREE

Vegan butter is one of those ingredients you always want in the fridge, whether you make your own or buy it. Whether you're making the topping for Apple Crisp French Toast Casserole (page 20) or mixing it into your Lemon-Basil Cauliflower Rice (page 43), you'll be glad you had it on hand!

½ cup unsweetened soy milk

2 teaspoons apple cider vinegar

1 cup refined coconut oil, melted

1 (14-ounce) can full-fat coconut milk, refrigerated overnight

¼ cup avocado oil

¾ teaspoon salt

⅛ teaspoon ground turmeric

1. In a bowl, whisk together the milk and vinegar and set aside to curdle for 4 to 5 minutes.

2. In a blender, combine the coconut oil and curdled milk. Carefully, without shaking or jostling it, open the can of coconut milk and scoop the solidified cream into the blender, along with the oil, salt, and turmeric. Blend until smooth.

3. Pour the mixture into 2 or 3 small glass bowls, cover, and refrigerate for at least 1 hour before using.

MAKE AHEAD: Your butter will stay fresh refrigerated in an airtight container for up to 2 weeks. I recommend doubling the recipe (and using twice as many small containers for fast chilling) so you always have some on hand!

MOUTHWATERING SEITAN "MEAT"

SERVES 8 / PREP TIME: 15 minutes, plus up to 1 hour to chill / **COOK TIME:** 45 minutes

NUT-FREE / SOY-FREE

I rarely buy mock meats because this seitan is so versatile: you can slice it and make Super Smoky Seitan Bacon (page 149), chop it and make Chick'n Noodle Soup (page 59), or run it through your food processor to make meaty crumbles.

1½ cups vital wheat gluten

⅓ cup nutritional yeast

¼ cup chickpea flour

1½ teaspoons poultry or chicken seasoning

1 teaspoon garlic powder

1 teaspoon salt

½ teaspoon paprika

½ teaspoon ground cumin

½ teaspoon onion powder

1½ cups vegetable broth, chilled

1. In a large bowl, combine the vital wheat gluten, nutritional yeast, chickpea flour, poultry seasoning, garlic powder, salt, paprika, cumin, and onion powder. Whisk until completely mixed.

2. Create a well in the middle and add the broth. Using a silicone spatula, stir until the mixture pulls away from the sides of the bowl and forms a dough.

3. Knead the dough for 3 to 4 minutes, until it thickens and firms. Move the dough to a cutting board and form into a rectangle shape. Let the dough rest for 10 minutes. Knead for another 30 seconds, then cut the dough into 4 equal loaves. Wrap each loaf in a 6-inch-wide piece of aluminum foil, loosely but completely so the seitan has room to expand as it cooks.

〉〉

4. In a pot, bring about 1 inch of water to a simmer. Place the seitan loaves in a steamer basket or insert and set the steamer in the pot, ensuring the water isn't touching the seitan. Cover and steam for 30 to 45 minutes, until the top of the seitan loaves feel semi-firm to the touch. If the loaves are crowded in the basket, rotate them around after the first 15 minutes.

5. Remove the seitan from the steamer and let the loaves cool for a few minutes before removing them from the foil. Refrigerate for 30 to 60 minutes, or until completely cool, before storing in air-tight containers until ready to use.

MAKE AHEAD: Wrapped tightly in a plastic bag, this seitan freezes wonderfully for up to 3 months.

SUPER SMOKY SEITAN BACON

SERVES 4 / **PREP TIME:** 10 minutes, plus 30 minutes to marinate / **COOK TIME:** 8 minutes

NUT-FREE

This bacon is crispy and chewy and smoky and maple-y, all at the same time. It is truly some of the best vegan bacon I've ever tasted! It'll fry up crispy or chewy, depending on how thin or thick your slices are.

⅓ cup soy sauce

¼ cup real maple syrup

1 tablespoon smoked paprika

½ teaspoon garlic powder

½ teaspoon black pepper

2 loaves Mouthwatering Seitan "Meat" (page 147)

6 teaspoons olive oil

1. In a shallow bowl, whisk together the soy sauce, maple syrup, smoked paprika, garlic powder, and pepper. Slice the seitan lengthwise into 8 to 10 thin slices, depending on the size of your loaf. Place the slices in the soy sauce mix and marinate for 30 minutes.

2. In a large skillet, heat 1 teaspoon of oil over medium heat until hot. Working in batches to avoid crowding, add the seitan to the pan in a single layer and drizzle a few spoonfuls of the remaining marinade over the top. Cook for 2 to 4 minutes on each side, adding more marinade as desired, or until crispy and browned.

3. Repeat with the remaining seitan and oil. Let cool for a minute or so before serving.

    VARIATION: If you're watching your salt intake, use reduced-sodium soy sauce. There is already some salt in the seitan itself for flavor.

MEASUREMENT CONVERSIONS

VOLUME EQUIVALENTS (LIQUID)

US STANDARD	US STANDARD (OUNCES)	METRIC (APPROXIMATE)
2 tablespoons	1 fl. oz.	30 mL
¼ cup	2 fl. oz.	60 mL
½ cup	4 fl. oz.	120 mL
1 cup	8 fl. oz.	240 mL
1½ cups	12 fl. oz.	355 mL
2 cups or 1 pint	16 fl. oz.	475 mL
4 cups or 1 quart	32 fl. oz.	1 L
1 gallon	128 fl. oz.	4 L

OVEN TEMPERATURES

FAHRENHEIT (F)	CELSIUS (C) (APPROXIMATE)
250° F	120° C
300° F	150° C
325° F	165° C
350° F	180° C
375° F	190° C
400° F	200° C
425° F	220° C
450° F	230° C

VOLUME EQUIVALENTS (DRY)

US STANDARD	METRIC (APPROXIMATE)
⅛ teaspoon	0.5 mL
¼ teaspoon	1 mL
½ teaspoon	2 mL
¾ teaspoon	4 mL
1 teaspoon	5 mL
1 tablespoon	15 mL
¼ cup	59 mL
⅓ cup	79 mL
½ cup	118 mL
⅔ cup	156 mL
¾ cup	177 mL
1 cup	235 mL
2 cups or 1 pint	475 mL
3 cups	700 mL
4 cups or 1 quart	1 L
½ gallon	2 L
1 gallon	4 L

WEIGHT EQUIVALENTS

US STANDARD	METRIC (APPROXIMATE)
½ ounce	15 g
1 ounce	30 g
2 ounces	60 g
4 ounces	115 g
8 ounces	225 g
12 ounces	340 g
16 ounces or 1 pound	455 g

INDEX

ACKNOWLEDGMENTS

Writing a cookbook is always a challenge, but as it turns out, it's even more so during a pandemic! So, while I'm always thankful to my sous-chef Denise Lindom, and to Mom and Bobby for being my #1 taste-testers, this time I'm also grateful to all my friends and family and readers who kept my spirits buoyed when it felt like I had taken on a tiny bit too much. Thank you Eric Bergman and Chelsea Stromberg for creating the funniest text group ever, and thank you Sharon Meyer for the hikes and smiles and silly memes. Also, thank you to my sister-in-law Kathy and all the helpful neighbors for sewing masks to help keep me safe during all those trips to the grocery store!

An enormous thank you to my testing team, who wouldn't let a quarantine or empty grocery shelves stop them! Susan and Erin Burgmaier (whom I refer to as the Dynamic Duo of recipe testing), Brooke Dunn, Sherri "SherBear" Maxwell, Cynthia Thayer, and Mandy Zila—you all rock! Not only could I not have done this without you, I wouldn't have wanted to. Your feedback and insights were so helpful, and I'm grateful for all the time and effort you contributed.

Last but definitely not least, thank you to everyone at Callisto Media, and especially to Van and Britt for your guidance and wisdom. I feel so lucky to have you all in my corner.

ABOUT THE AUTHOR

BARB MUSICK lives in Colorado with her pack of rescue pets. She shares her adventures and love of food, travel, and animals on her blog, *That Was Vegan?*, along with vegan recipes everyone will love. This is her fourth cookbook. Visit her at ThatWasVegan.com.

CPSIA information can be obtained
at www.ICGtesting.com
Printed in the USA
JSHW051611300421
13898JS00001B/2

9 781648 760068